If God Were to Speak to You

This is what the Lord says …

Fidelma Hernon

Unless otherwise noted, all scripture quotations are from the New International Version of the Bible.

HOLY SPIRIT
BOOKS

Holy Spirit Books
173 Dolphin House
Dolphin Barn
South Circular Road
Dublin 8
D08 FD3A

For permission requests and speaking inquiries email info@holyspiritbooks.org.

ISBN: 978-1-9192062-0-2 (Paperback)
ISBN: 978-1-9192062-1-9 (Hardcover)
ISBN: 978-1-9192062-2-6 (eBook)

Book design, proofreading, and formatting by Transcendent Publishing.

Dedication

This book is dedicated to all the lost people
who believe God has forgotten them.
I was one of those lost people.

May the Lord bless you
through this book.

God bless you,
Fidelma

Contents

Psalm 23

The LORD is my shepherd, I lack nothing.
He makes me lie down in green pastures,
He leads me beside quiet waters,
He refreshes my soul.
He guides me along the right paths
for His name's sake.
Even though I walk
through the darkest valley,
I will fear no evil,
for you are with me;
your rod and your staff,
they comfort me.

You prepare a table before me
in the presence of my enemies.
You anoint my head with oil;
my cup overflows.
Surely your goodness and love will follow me
all the days of my life,
and I will dwell in the house of the LORD
forever.

Preface

Psalm 23:1

*"The Lord is my shepherd,
I lack nothing."*

At seventeen years of age, I was directionless after leaving school. I gave my life to the Lord during a private conversation with God. This was a spiritual act, but I didn't know that at the time. There were many decades following this dedication, during which I thought God had forgotten about me. Then I had an encounter with the Holy Spirit which changed everything. On first attending a small prayer group, the Holy Spirit came upon me. I began to weep.

It was not a sorrowful weeping, but one full of overwhelming peace, love, comfort, and joy. I received such deep reassurance from the Holy Spirit. When the people prayed for me, God shared things from my life with them, and I knew that God had always known me, always been with me, always watched over me. However, I had questioned it many, many times!

I attended a Bible study and started reading the Bible. Having discovered that God had promised me peace, joy, health, provision for all my needs, and had plans for my life, I began to apply these promises to my life. To my surprise, it began to change, and I had victory in many difficult situations. The Holy Spirit then released a gift in me to speak in tongues and the ability to translate what was spoken.

This book consists of the answers God has given me when I have prayed in tongues for myself and others.

God has not forgotten you. He is shepherding you quietly, just as he did me. He will speak to you in this book. May the following pages reveal the sweet love God the Father, Jesus, and the Holy Spirit have for you. I pray that you open your heart to receive the peace, protection, comfort, joy, and love that the Father aches to give you.

Foreword

The first time I met Fidelma over ten years ago, I spoke the Words of the Bible to her. In my twenty-five years of Bible teaching, I have never seen anyone devour the Word like she did. She snatched it out of my hand. Fidelma had been searching and searching and was famished in the wilderness. However, once she experienced the Holy Spirit and heard the Word of God, it was like a great hunger came to the surface; she didn't know she had. Fidelma hooked her sail to God's boat, and he rescued her. She put her hope in God and never let him go.

In her early years as a baby Christian in the Kingdom, Fidelma was diligent on her path with the Lord. No longer searching in the darkness, she now searched the Word with the light turned on in her for guidance with every step she took. Many, many times, she questioned which step to take but always pressed into the Lord for the answer.

Fidelma has certainly walked through the valley of darkness. I have been a witness to the relentless battles she has gone through. Battles were coming from all directions. Over time, Fidelma began to see that the Lord was in control as long as she let him, his plan always prevailed, even if it didn't look like it. After the battles, her spiritual growth became more and more evident. It was apparent in her deep understanding of the Bible and the incredible revelation God has given her.

The Lord did a mighty work in Fidelma, restoring and renewing her in him. He anointed her with a wonderful gift of prophecy, which pours out of her belly. Over the last three years, many people in our church have been blessed to receive these prophecies when Fidelma has prayed for them. The beautiful part is that God speaks directly to the person who needs the prayer, and Fidelma does not know the details revealed in the prophecy. Fidelma has become very sensitive to hearing the Holy Spirit, expressed in the sweet prophecies collected in this book.

I am absolutely thrilled that this book is now available to everyone. It contains the anointing of God in such a simple way. It will speak to every person who needs a Word in season from the Lord. It will soothe every wounded soul. It is a precious gift of encouragement, hope, and love for anyone who needs it … And we all need it.

Stephen O'Brien
Minister of the Living Word
(@the livingword999)

Introduction

This book, conceived in God's heart, came through me to your heart. God didn't tell me I was writing a book until it was almost finished. I guess he didn't need my opinion!! All he needed was my obedience! The verses you are about to read came together over three years. When I pray in tongues for myself or others, the Holy Spirit gives me the translation. At first, he gave me three words. When I wrote them down, he then gave me three more words, and eventually it became phrases and sentences.

When I was a new Christian visiting a relative in the hospital, I visited its chapel and picked up a little card, and written on it was Psalm 23:1a, "The Lord is my shepherd." Later, one morning I came home from working the night shift in my laboratory job and was worried about a situation at work. I went to the Lord, and initially nothing was working, but he led me to Psalm 23, written on the card I had placed next to my bed.

As soon as I started to read it, the power of God instantly came over me as a blanket of peace, comfort, reassurance, and love. It was the first time I experienced the power of the Word of God. It was truly incredible. Since that day, I have spoken this Psalm almost every day.

As I started to put together the collection of verses for this book, the Holy Spirit said the book would take the form of the journey as described in Psalm 23. It was only then that I realized that I had been living Psalm 23 and that the Lord was truly my shepherd.

I walked through the valley of darkness for most of my life without God. I was in my fourth decade before I had an encounter with the Holy Spirit. I continued to walk through the valley of darkness, but now I had company: God the Father, Jesus, and the Holy Spirit. Over time, I learned to surrender to the Almighty. To have peace, even when he closed the doors I wanted to go through and opened the doors I didn't want to go through.

Now, after ten years walking with the Lord, when I surrender a situation to the Lord but begin to debate the problem in my head, I say, "Sorry, Lord. I surrender that situation to you again." I am still a work in progress! But I look back at my life before, and now it is entirely different. I am filled with peace, joy, and freedom. I do not want. I receive victory after victory in every situation. This is available to everyone!

I see many women around me pouring out everything they have to their careers, families, and communities, but there is a vacancy inside them that only God can fill. A supernatural thirst that cannot be filled in the flesh or in the natural, but only in the supernatural. It is no coincidence you are reading this book; the Lord has drawn you to him. There is nothing to lose but everything to gain as you take this sweet journey with the Lord as your shepherd.

This book is not just a book to read, it is an experience!

Bonus

If you would like to record your journey with the Lord through this book, please go to www.holyspiritbooks.org for a free download of **My Journey Out of the Valley of Darkness**, where you can write down your experiences and encounters with the Lord. Create your own book!

Chapter 1

The Valley of Darkness – In the Wilderness

Psalm 23:4

"Even though I walk
through the darkest valley . . ."

Throughout my life, I have had many valleys of darkness as described in Psalm 23.

Many years ago, while studying abroad, nothing seemed to work out. Everything was difficult—family, friends, relationships, and my studies. I couldn't control or manage everything, so each day, I focused on what I could do well that day. Eventually, everything resolved itself, and I completed my studies successfully. I didn't think God was with me, but now I know he was always there.

Whatever family, community, or profession you may be from, there is a time in everyone's life when you don't know which way to turn. You cannot see the road ahead due to the darkness. You may feel isolated, excluded, abused, with no one to talk to, no one to confide in. The Lord wants you to know that he hears you, sees you, and aches for you to cry out to him. The Father is drawing you to him now.

Cry in the Shadows

This is what the Lord says ... I see you cry in the shadows. I see the cry of your heart; it has an open wound and bleeding love. You try to cover it up and hide it, but I see it, your broken heart. It is time for you to let my love pour into your wounds and soothe your aching soul. I have all that you need. I have a new heart for you, one crafted by me. Do not stay in the shadows any longer but come into the light and let me put my arms around you, and you can rest, for I will take all your burdens, all your weariness upon me.

Whisper

This is what the Lord says ... I am here, says the Lord. I hear your cry. I see your pain. I answer. Though you do not receive the answer I send, for you don't know me. You don't know my ways, don't recognize my voice, and don't receive from me. I am sending someone now who will open your eyes, open your ears, and, most importantly, open your heart to me. You will at last invite me in, and I will enjoy your company, and you will enjoy mine.

You will recognize my voice, identify my ways, and receive the answers to your prayers that I send. You will grow in faith, know my Word, grow and develop in the spirit, and your faith will be strong. You will no longer cry out, no longer suffer in pain. But when required, you will whisper to me on the inside, and I will whisper back.

Fear and Strife

This is what the Lord says ... I have allowed things to happen to wake up my children. My children have everything available to them. All the protection of heaven is available to you but you do not receive it. The door has been opened to the pestilence. It will go on until my children call on me. There is no peace in the land. There is only fear and strife. I long to pour out my peace, but my children reject it. I am doing a new thing. I am raising up brothers and sisters to stand and point the direction to me, to peace and refuge. Call me, my children, and I will answer.

Come with Me

This is what the Lord says ... I am calling you to me. I am calling you out of the wilderness into the promised land. Come with me. The Egyptians continually looked back, and it took forty years before only two of them came into the promised land. Stop looking back. Look to me. Look to what I have promised you. Don't believe the lies any longer, believe the truth. The truth shall set you free.

Run to Me

This is what the Lord says... I moan and groan for my children. They run from me, but I want them to run to me. They don't see me, but I see them. Soon they will see me because of you, my child—my child, so highly favored. They will see my healing hands. They will see my healing heart. They will see how I clear the paths for them. They will feel my love. They will see my power, and they will feel my glory. All coming through you, my child.

I have called many, but few answer. I instruct many, but few are obedient. But you give me all, you surrender yourself more and more. And because of this, you are highly favored. Favor will follow you everywhere, and I will open the doors I want opened for you. Thank you, my child.

Loving and Compassionate

This is what the Lord says... I am in charge. I see the failure of people to trust me and depend on me. When you don't depend on me, you depend on the devil. I am bringing you out of the shadows. You will be my light. You will astound all around you by what you do through me. You will honor me with glory, and in time, everyone around you will do that. The world will see that I am a good, loving, compassionate God who wants to bless my children. They will want to know me because of you.

You Pluck, I Pluck

This is what the Lord says ... Your fingers are my fingers. As you pluck your guitar, I pluck mine. We are one, you and I. Your heart is my heart. It is a jewel full of glory. But your mind has not been set on me—distracted by worldly things and lied to by the enemy. When the enemy speaks to you and your mind is confused, come to me when you are weary and brokenhearted. For I pour into you the soothing love from heaven from my heart, and I will tell you the truth.

My heart has ached for you to be close to me again. My ears yearn to hear you sing to me again. Come close, my dear son, for it is safe here with me.

Tug of War

This is what the Lord says ...Everything I do for you, I do for love. There is a tug of war going on. One side is love, the other is hate. My love softens while hate hardens. My arms are warm, but the enemies are cold. I am forever calling you closer and closer that I may embrace you. There is no circumstance in which I can't draw you closer to me. There is no test the enemy can test you with that you cannot win, overcome, or have the victory.

Victories are always available to you. Just as my heart is set on you, your heart must be set on Jesus. He has bought the victory for you. Settle into the hope that I have provided for you. Cling to that hope. You have taken up your position. Now stand firm and see the deliverance I will give you. After this test, you will come forth as gold.

Trust Path

This is what the Lord says ... I see you in the desert places. I bring the water to you to refresh you, to enlighten you to the things available to you in the kingdom. The kingdom is all around you. You just have to step into it and continue to walk in it, rejecting the world's lies. For I have created an invisible world around you, but you can see the unseen through me. Your tongue opens the door into the invisible.

As you trust in me and step inside the door, you will see the invisible become visible. I have a ring of fire around you. There is nothing to lose but everything to gain when trusting me. I bring you my Son, Peace, and he releases the chains to the world, which frees you to take the step through the door. Everyone can speak words, but are you going to accompany your words with action, take the step onto the trust path?

Come Home

This is what the Lord says ... I look around, searching for my lost loved ones. I am looking, calling, searching to bring them home. I have a heaven prepared for their arrival. All the angels know who you are. We have an expectant home here in heaven, expectant of family of brothers and sisters. Before you were born, I prepared this place for you. So sad that many never come home. They leave like emigrants, but some never return home. I desire that all people return home to where they belong. It is the cry of my heart for my children to come home to me. I long for it. Brothers and sisters, help your lost brothers and sisters come home to be a family once again.

Rescue Boat

This is what the Lord says ... I created my children to flourish and reproduce. It is the natural cycle of life. The animal kingdom has stayed closer to the natural cycle than mankind has. Yet, man has been blessed far greater than the animal kingdom. My children have been created to reproduce. But the devil has come against it in many ways, killing babies, the elderly, and now also the sick. When I have provided everything that is needed for my children, it saddens me to see the pain suffered and the pain inflicted.

My children chose the devil's path instead of my path. But I am raising you up and others who will be the lights that line the path, showing my children where to go and how to go. You, as my lights, are directing them to the light where they will be with me. The devil's path only leads to darkness, further pain, and destruction. Darkness in this life leads to further eternal darkness. Light in this life leads to further eternal life.

I have already rescued you, my children, by sending my Son, Jesus. The boat has pulled up alongside you to take you out of the drifting current, but you refuse to get in. You call on me, but reject the answer to your prayer. I send the boat many times, but you do not get in. I plead with you, but you don't come. You don't hear me. Come and know me so you may recognize my voice, so that you might know the voice of your Father calling you into the boat.

Big Brother Jesus

This is what the Lord says ... My eyes are on my children all the time. I do not blink in case I miss something. I see every move, every beat of your heart, every thought you think, every word you speak, every laugh you laugh, and every tear you cry, as we are one in spirit. I am aware of everything within you and everything around you. I want to swoop down, cradle you in my arms, and soothe your weary soul with my love.

But most of all, I want you strong and full of the peace my Son, your brother Jesus, has provided for you. If I overstepped my boundary and took you away from trouble, then the sacrifice

Jesus made would be in vain. He has provided peace, strength, wisdom, joy, and freedom for you. You are an overcomer and always have the victory in Jesus. I cannot steal that from you by not allowing you to grow up. He is your big brother. And if you hold his hand, he will look after you and take you places beyond where your imagination is now.

Life in Abundance

This is what the Lord says ... I open your eyes. I see through you into your heart. Your eyes only see me from a distance, only the periphery of me. I call you into me now to abide in me and I in you so you can see me in full glory. I open your eyes to show you the heart of me. The heart I have for you and my children. How I long to pour my love into you to heal the wounds of the past and free you from the bondage of the enemy that you may live life in abundance, just as Jesus has provided for you.

Divine Exchange

This is what the Lord says ... I see your heart, your broken heart. I have the love that can fill that open wound and stitch it up. You seek me in other places, but I am right here. You come and go; your visits with me are fleeting. Come and stay a bit longer, that I may do a work within you, that I may nurture, comfort, and heal you to bring you to a place that I may build your life up around you and bless you in all areas of your life. You do not need to struggle as you do. Give it to me, and there will be a divine exchange where I give you a blessing for every struggle you give me. Know that I love you, and it is unchanging and steadfast forever.

Cup of Trust

This is what the Lord says ... Your thirst is for me. Your hunger is for the bread I provide. Come to me for your needs. Come to me for all things, for I will give you the desires of your heart. I will provide you with all things for your enjoyment. I will add no sorrow to it. Drink from the cup of trust that Jesus has provided for you. Surrender all to me so I may move into all areas of your heart and life. Do not resist my love for you. The love I can give you cannot be compared.

Your Journey – Step Number One

I hope you have drawn closer to the Father through his loving words. This is the beginning of an incredible, special journey of healing and restoration for you. To document this historic event in your life, please go to www.holyspiritbooks.org for a free download of **My Journey Out of the Valley of Darkness**. There, you can record the journey by answering the questions suggested. Create a personal memoir of the discovery of the Father and inevitably discover your true self as the Lord sees you, as he draws out of you the person he created you to be.

Chapter 2

The Lord is My Shepherd – Coming into the Light

Psalm 23:1

"The Lord is my Shepherd,
I lack nothing."

At seventeen years of age, I gave my life to God. Although I didn't know it, I made the Lord the Shepherd of my life that day. I didn't know if I was good at anything or what I was supposed to do with my life. Somehow, I knew that God knew, he had a plan I couldn't see. I told God he would have to make what he wanted me to do obvious. I asked him to close the doors he didn't want me to go through and only open the door he did want me to go through. I didn't want to mess up his plan! Although I didn't know it then, if I had started to read the Bible and gotten to know the Father and Jesus, he would have revealed his plans to me.

The Father has drawn you here to introduce you to his son Jesus. In John 6.44a Jesus said, "No one can come to me unless the Father who sent me draws them ..." Jesus is called the

"Word of God" in Revelation 19:13, "He is dressed in a robe dipped in blood, and his name is the Word of God."

Jesus, also known as "the Word," will come into the valley of darkness to be with you; he is the light that lights up the path. Psalm 119:105 "Your word is a lamp for my feet, a light on my path." He will show you the direction to go, you will not be afraid, he will protect and comfort you. Psalm 23:4 "Even though I walk through the darkest valley, I will fear no evil, for you are with me; your rod and your staff, they comfort me."

We may wish that the Father would remove us from the challenging situations in our lives, instead, he sends a rescuer, Jesus. Jesus shows us the way out of the valley of darkness, protects us, offers us relief from our problems, and comforts us as we walk.

Walk with Jesus

This is what the Lord says … All my children around the world are searching for me. They look here, there, and everywhere. However, they do not truly seek me out. I am available to all, but few come and stay with me. You have sought me out. You have come to me and remain with me, walking alongside my Son, Jesus. Jesus says, "I am blessed to walk with you, for my Father's love has laid the path on which we walk. He has created all that is available, but it is through me that it is available. What you have sought to obtain, you have obtained through me. All of the abundance of heaven and earth is available to you through me by just receiving my spirit and resting in me."

True Success

This is what the Lord says ... Every time you turn to me, I turn to you. I lift you up over my shoulders. I am raising you up. I hold you up high as I take each step up the stairs of success. I carry you. True success in life is to have your name written in the book of life, the book of eternal life. You have not secured your place in heaven if your name is not written in this book. There is a place for everyone, but not everyone receives it.

Accepting my Son, Jesus is the only way to me, the only way to secure your future, true success. Although everyone knows you cannot take anything from this world into the next. Yet they deny the truth, they reject Jesus. You, my child, will show them the way to true success, true freedom. You will do that with my Son, Jesus, carrying you up the stairs of success according to how the world knows it. People plan for retirement, but they do not plan beyond that. When they leave the earth, they leave everything behind— plan for eternal life in heaven.

Yoke for Yoke

This is what the Lord says ... My love, you have been away from me for so long. Always busy. Be busy with me? Come to me, says the Lord. You are weary and burdened. Let me unburden you. Take my yoke, and I will take your yoke. We have done this before. Now let us do it again. I want for you to live a gentle, peaceful life full of the fruit of the Spirit. Not full of the fruit of the world. Let me take your yoke. Rest in me and allow grace to carry you through all your endeavors. I want my little child back on my lap, singing to me.

Surrendered

This is what the Lord says ... Your future is in my hands. You have put it in my hands. You've given me the freedom to mold and sculpt you into the person I have created you to be. Your future will be full of powerful, extraordinary events, as I will orchestrate, but executed by you. You have an ear for my voice, an ear for my instruction. Through this obedience, your future will be outstanding in a class of its own, all because you allowed me into you and your life.

Smile

This is what the Lord says ... I was waiting for you to wake, to give you good news. I waited that I might smile on you. Today is deliverance day. You have cast all your cares onto me, and now I can remove the enemy's yoke on you. This is the time of freedom, and freedom is delivered to you. You have delivered to me the yoke of the enemy, and in the divine exchange, I deliver freedom to you. Next is a time of blessings.

Written on your Heart

This is what the Lord says ... My written Word is the promise. I have written the promises on your heart, for out of the heart flow the issues of life. Once the Words leave your lips, they come to my heart. Our hearts are in agreement; when two are in agreement, it is established.

Blindfolded

This is what the Lord says ... I am doing a new thing. The old has passed away. You are renewed in me. You are blindfolded right now. You do not see the steps of the path in front of you. But I am right next to you, guiding you. You will come to a place in the path when I take the blindfold off, and you will be amazed at where you are. Right now, keep doing what you are doing. Keep your ear alert for me, and you will see the fruit of your walk very soon.

The Journey

This is what the Lord says ... I recognize your queries and concerns, for I see the world's chaos and the devil's schemes—a cobweb of deceit and lies to entangle, distract, and abuse my children. But I sent my Son, who is the spirit of freedom so that my children will tear down all those systems of entrapment that bind and prevent them from flourishing and releasing the fruits of their Spirit.

I have called many children to labor with me on the farm. However, there are few laborers, and the harvest is small. Yet, even one great laborer can produce a plentiful harvest. Many will turn and look and ask, *How?* For they cannot see. First, they must hear, then, when they apply the Word, they will see. How blessed are you to collaborate with me all these years, yet have not seen the harvest.

But the soil is so rich, you have tended the Garden of Eden within you with tenderness, love, patience, and eagerness to do all you can. Soon, the fruit of that harvest will burst through you, and you will produce a crop a hundred times what you have sown. (Mark 4:20) You have declared it over and over, and you will have what you say. You heard me so clearly when I spoke to you through Jeremiah 29:14b "...

and will bring you back to the place from which I carried you into exile." I have brought you back to the Garden of Eden, where you co-labor with me. You have a joyful spirit as you rest in the garden with me.

Isaiah 12:3 says, "With joy you will draw water from the wells of salvation." For many years, the spirit of oppression has stifled your progress. But now you are strong, and that spirit has no place in you, and its effect will be no more. You will strive forward unhindered, and I will give you every place you set your foot. Goodness and love will follow you. Joy overtakes you, but I surround you. And every step you take, you step into the footprint that I have made, for I go before you and make the way clear for my child who I love dearly.

Petals

This is what the Lord says ... I have picked you out of a pond where the lilies grow. I brought you to an unfamiliar place where the ground is hard for you to take root in. But I have covered you with a layer of favor, and the ground will open up and receive you, and you will take root again. When this happens, you will flourish like nothing seen before. Your life is like a flower with many petals, but I am holding the flower.

Building Your House

This is what the Lord says ... First, I will build you up, build you up like a tower people will run to. Once you are built up, you can build others. How can a builder who only knows how to build half a house instruct others on how to build their houses? Your house is solid and strong, but not complete. I am refining and fine-tuning. I am looking at the details. When you are complete, then I will open your doors. Others will take shelter and refuge in you as you take shelter and refuge in me. You are made in my image and likeness. (Genesis 1:27)

Apple of My Eye

This is what the Lord says ... My eye is on you. My eye follows you wherever you go. I cannot take my eyes off you. You are the apple of my eye. When I reveal you, others will look on you as I do. I see my glory in you, and they will see it in you, too. Some will reject it and be afraid, but many will come to my glory. I will be like a magnet to the lost, a safe house. I will be the food for the hungry, for they have been spiritually starved. It is time for a feast for the spirit to build up and to be strong again in me, says the Lord.

Peeling the Layers

This is what the Lord says ... I am the light. (John 8:12) You are the light. (Matt 5:14-16) I send you out like a torch. People see you from their darkness. They see that you are different. They don't know what to do with you. But I know. I know the plans I have for you. (Jeremiah 29:11) I will peel off the layers. And gradually they will see me and you. They won't know what is happening, but it will amaze them. You have a great secret treasure within you, and I am peeling back the layers to reveal it. You have such peace and joy as I do this for you. Know it is truly I and not you being revealed. There will be chaos around you, but you will remain in perfect peace.

Light

This is what the Lord says ... I am growing you up to be the light for me. I've placed a treasure within you. It has been buried for a long time, but I am unveiling it, removing the covers the enemy has put on it. This light is pure and nourishing to the soul and body. It will feed many and heal many. They will look to you, and through you will see me. This is all I have ever wanted for my children—to see my glory and come to me. Hold fast now, for the final layers are coming off. The stronger you hold onto me, the faster it will happen. The revelation is near, hold fast.

Jewel in My Heart

This is what the Lord says ... You are the jewel in my heart, precious beyond words. You have suffered greatly, though your heart always belonged to me. It was my voice you did not hear. My hands, you did not see. But now you hear and see me. And I have supernatural blessings for you and your family. Your prayers are heard. Now that we are together, let us never be parted, for I have a greater purpose for your life. The beginnings are already being expressed through you. But this is only the beginning. So, have high expectations of me, and I will bring you far.

Fruit of the Spirit

This is what the Lord says ... I am rising within you, breaking off the attachments to worldly things. You have set your heart upon me, but the breaking off can be painful and requires patience and endurance. These I have given you in abundance, for these are the characteristics which are needed for me to shape and sculpt you. But the fruit of the pruning will be joyous. You will be so filled with joy that the process will have been well worth it. Few walk this walk with me, but you will continue, just as others see the fruits of decades of prayer and calling out to me. Likewise, you will see the harvest. The harvest will be so plentiful that it will spill over to many others. The fruit of the Spirit will overflow and touch many people. For I am God, and my plan for you will come to pass.

The Word Becomes Flesh

This is what the Lord says ... My eyes, heart, and hands are open to you. All that I have, I give to you; the blessings of heaven are upon you. You cannot fail. I have given you all I have on the inside that you might battle on the outside. I have given you the armor, the sword, and the roadmap to your success. Use what I have given you. Things only seen in the spirit will be seen in the flesh.

Cornerstone of My Body

This is what the Lord says ... My little toe on my right foot was knitted together in my mother's womb, where it was nurtured and grew. As I grew up, so did my little toe take on a heavy burden, being the cornerstone of my body. This tiny digit takes my body's weight, keeping me upright and balanced. I can go up and down on it, making myself taller when I want to. This little toe gets strapped into sandals, squeezed into shoes. When it finally gets freedom, it gets hit against furniture or walks into something sharp. It is happiest on soft grass or sand at the beach.

But this is a blessed toe. Created by the mighty hand of God, whose heavenly breath blew life into it. The DNA of almighty God is in it, the blood of Jesus runs through it, and it is dressed with a beautiful nail. It is a strong and mighty member of my body. Fighting off attempts by the enemy to attack my body. But Jesus is in my little toe. The Word penetrates my little toe, and it responds to the Word. All you need for victory is the Word and love.

Sometimes I forget about my little toe. It doesn't get any attention during the everyday routine. But you are my rock on which I stand, a cornerstone of my body. Thank you, my little toe. I will not forget to send love to you again, my little toe. Just as Jesus is the cornerstone of your spirit, your little toe is the cornerstone of your body.

A Ribbon Called Jesus

This is what the Lord says ... I am in you, and you are in me. I have placed in you a treasure chest full of treasures from my heart. As I open that chest, the treasures come to life. They are coming to life by the Word you are speaking. Each treasure is wrapped in a ribbon called Jesus. As you continue to open up your mind, body, and soul to me, I can release further treasures, and you become more and more like my Son, Jesus. These treasures are the desires of my heart for you, your family, all those around you, and nations around the world. Continue your walk with my Son, Jesus. And as you release these treasures, the desires of your heart and mine will come to be.

He Gathers Chicks

This is what the Lord says ... I am the creator of all, nothing comes upon the earth except through my Son, Jesus. Everything has been thought of, considered valuable, and created. The smallest of creatures have biological systems that only God could create. I am that God; there is only one God. All other gods are false. The enemy tries to create poor imitations of me, but with no life. For I am eternal life, everything I create has eternal life in it. Though the body may fail, the spirit is pure, and the soul belongs to me.

I gather my children around me as a hen gathers her chicks to protect and nurture them, to grow them up in my image and likeness, and to surrender their hearts to me so that I may move through them. The greater the surrender, the more I can step into their lives and the greater the victory.

The Kingdom Inside

This is what the Lord says ... I am living on the inside of you. Inside is where the kingdom is, and outside is where the world is. My kingdom flows out of you as living water. The world rejects my living water, but it seeps its way into the souls who hunger for me and cry out to me. For I hear my children cry, and I answer them. I have sent them an exact representation of me to show them the way to me—my Son, Jesus.

Your Journey – Step Number Two

This can be a new direction for your life. A direction where you don't have to carry all the burden and figure everything out. It is a road where Jesus is available to you to cast all your fears and concerns onto him, allow him to be your friend, and lead you on a new road that you would go. No longer are you alone. Record your personal journey on the road of life before meeting Jesus and how it has been changed by Jesus joining you on your road of life by reviewing the questions in the Bonus gift.

Chapter 3

He Restores My Soul – Heals My Wounds

Psalm 23:2-3

"He makes me lie down in green pastures,
He leads me beside quiet waters,
He refreshes my soul."

Words and events shape our lives and profoundly impact us. It can be difficult to see our wounds and how we operate from that wounded place. But as I took the path with Jesus, he showed me how wounded other people were. The Lord began to show me people through his eyes. People who were difficult to interact with, I could see that it was a reaction to a deep wound within them. They weren't attacking me, but screaming on the inside from the pain they were in. Instead of feeling I had to protect myself from people, I now had empathy. As the Lord gave me this insight and I responded to it, he, in turn, was healing me.

As we live in the world, we get battered physically, mentally, and emotionally by many events and words spoken over us. Many scars and wounds can persist, and we can develop particular defensive habits to protect those seeping wounds. As we journey through the valley of darkness, the Lord wants to pour his healing love into those wounds, soothe and nurture you in those painful places in your heart, body, and mind, so that you can be free and allow him to protect you from this day forward.

Bleeding Heart

This is what the Lord says ... I see the cries of your heart, the pain and wounds that have made your heart bleed. It continues to bleed. I want to pour my love into those open wounds so they may heal. I will stitch up those wounds just as I knit you together in your mother's womb. Let my love pour into you; it will wash away the unwanted things that hurt you. Let peace and joy come alive in you.

Tender Spot

This is what the Lord says ... I see the tender part of your heart that you protect fiercely. A strong cage surrounds it. Let me take those bars down. Let me heal that tender spot. It results from other people's failings and actions, not your own. All my children have tender spots in their hearts. The time has come for yours to be healed. Let me bathe your heart in my love so it may overflow. You are my precious child whom I love with all my heart. Let me give you my heart to replace your wounded heart, which may be continually filled with peace, joy, and security.

True Dad

This is what the Lord says ... I knit you in your mother's womb. You came from my imagination. I created you with my Word. I do not make mistakes. I operate within the laws of the spiritual realm, not the laws of the world, for I have created you for a great purpose. Move closer to me so that you may know the plans I have for you. For out of the ashes of the world, I create beauty. (Isaiah 61:3) You are that beauty. You are so beautiful to me; you are my baby girl, and I am your Father. I've watched over you all your life and have longed for you to know your true Dad, your Father in heaven.

Cast Your Cares

This is what the Lord says ... I hold your heart in my hand like a delicate flower. I cover it to protect it. I breathe life and love back into it so that the deep wounds of the past may be healed, and it will be like new again. I have surrounded you with people I want in your life, but there is so much noise and distraction. There is no peace. I want to place my peace in your heart. Be still and let my peace rest inside you, for you are my child. Now you are mine, and I look after my own. Come to me for all you need. Cast your cares onto me that you may soak in the freedom my Son, Jesus, has provided for you.

Thorns

This is what the Lord says ... My child loves me like no other. You bless me day and night, night and day. There is nothing I wouldn't do for you, who wakes with me and sleeps with me. The abundant gift I have put in you knows no bounds. But I see thorns surrounding that gift, holding it down, pinning it down like a pincushion, preventing it from inflating fully. Ask me to remove those thorns so that I may rise within you, and you may rise within me.

Delicate Flower

This is what the Lord says ... You are a delicate flower in my hand. The wind blows, and it flutters your petals. Your stem is bending, it sways to and fro all the time, my beautiful flower. You do not rest in me. You do not stay still to hear me whisper how I love you into your ear. When you rest in me, I can bring my arms around you and shield you from the storms surrounding you. My delicate, precious flower ... Your father loves you so much and longs to protect you.

Coat of Love

This is what the Lord says ... I cover you with my love. It is a pure love, an impenetrable love that envelops you. Keep my coat of love on you to protect you from the elements of evil, to keep you warm, my love will protect your heart. Let it pour into you. Surrender yourself more and more to me so that my coat of love can seep into all the crevices of your body and mind. Take comfort in my coat of love and know I will never remove it.

Quiet Voice

This is what the Lord says ... You strive and strive to come close to me, but I have already found you. You don't need to look here, there, and everywhere to get close to me. I am close to you. I am right inside your heart. Just rest in me and allow my peace to dwell in you. Seek me for all things, and my quiet voice will be louder than the noise of the world.

Four Words

This is what the Lord says ... I gave Moses four words to speak to Pharoh: "Let my people go" so my people would be freed. (Exodus 9:1) Ten times I sent Moses to the Pharaoh, and ten times he repeated these words. All this time, I, the Lord, was building a treasure for my people. The Israelites would never have been freed if Moses had stopped after the ninth time. I have given you my Word, and I want you to speak it from your heart. And all the while, I am building a treasure. Do not grow weary in doing good for at the proper time, you will receive a harvest. (Galatians 6:9)

The Word, your Anchor

This is what the Lord says ... I rise within you. As you speak my Word, you elevate Jesus, my Son. As you elevate my Son, Jesus, the Spirit of God—my Spirit—rises within you as you meditate on my Word. It establishes the foundation of the Word within you as an anchor for your life. You will see the expression and manifestation of my Word in your life. As you allow my Word to be the new foundation of your life, the old foundation on which you had built your life—the world—will fade away.

Breath of Greatness

This is what the Lord says ... I breathe greatness into you when you speak my Word. It goes through your ears and into your belly. From there, I draw it back out. You have set your heart on training yourself in the Word, being an apt student and diligent in study. That you may not just know my will and my intentions, but that they become assimilated into your being. As your worldly ways crumble, my Word surges within you to replace the old ways. Your body, mind, and soul are becoming renewed, renewed with the ability and power of my greatness.

Obedience

This is what the Lord says ... I ask you to come, and you come. I will ask you to go forth, and you will do it. You give me such great pleasure as you are obedient. I long for my children to be obedient so that I may protect and love them. Your obedience will bring the Spirit of Obedience upon them. You and I will see greater obedience in the future, a longing in my children to be close to me—to know me and by knowing me, know themselves, how I made them, what they are made of. They are made of me. What is their purpose, and how it may be fulfilled? Many, many will come to me, all because of your obedience.

Jealous God

This is what the Lord says ... You are now the powerhouse hidden in me. When infirmity or disease comes knocking, it knows you speak the Word. This is the light switch that shines the light on the demonic. It has to flee. You may have to clean house and put the light on in every room by speaking the Word over all infirmity. Do not make anything demonic welcome in your home. For I am in you and you are in me. There is no place for the enemy in you, for I am a jealous God.

Sun Will Shine Again

This is what the Lord says ... I hold you up with my right hand. The devil tries to pull you down, but you are in my strong tower. You are safe there. You have established yourself there through my Word. The storm rages but cannot touch you unless you step out of my tower. Then the elements will have their way with you. You are hidden, established, and rooted in love; the battle is mine. The storm will pass as quickly and suddenly as it started, and the sun will shine again.

All of Me

This is what the Lord says ... I anoint you; I bless you. I give ALL of myself to you to be available to my children. Through you, I can change things. I can turn things upside down. I can turn things the right way up. You will not always see what I am doing or know my ways in every situation. But know that I am always there, ever present and ever available to you.

A Receiving Heart

This is what the Lord says ... You are looking for someone with the same wounds you had. You are a new creation now; all things have passed away. (2 Corinthians 5:17) Look no more. When I bring the man into your life, you will not be searching but receiving. He will be a blessing and not be wounded, and he will not see the old wounds of the old man in you. But he will see the new creation of freedom, joy, and love, which will be flowing out of your belly.

Foliage Around My Flower

This is what the Lord says ... I made you in my image and likeness. Though you don't see it now, it is deep within you. You hide from me, but I see you. I see right into your heart and the troubles that live there. Let me take those troubles and worries from you so that you may be free. I have gifted you my flower, your wife, to love and protect. As she blooms, you are to blossom too. You are the foliage around my flower that feeds the flower. Don't be left hidden underground as your flower blooms, for I have a great plan for you together. Plans to prosper and not to harm you. (Jeremiah 29:11) For you are my child made in my image and likeness. (Genesis 1:27)

Desire of Your Heart

This is what the Lord says ... I light you up. I am the fragrance around you. I am the words that leave you. I'm the compassion that pours from you. I am the love within you. You have allowed me in. And as you continue to surrender yourself to me, I can do greater things through you and reach many people, many more of my children. The pruning can be harsh, but the blossom has begun and the fruit will come. Prepare to see all you have asked of me. For I will answer every prayer, and every desire of your heart will be fulfilled.

The Secret Things

This is what the Lord says ... Looking through you, I see the world through the eyes of a woman. I see the steps you take and the steps you avoid. I see the deliberations that go on in your mind. Though you seek me in all things, the world tries to interfere with where you are going. But very soon you will see through my eyes. You will see things hidden; the secret things I want to give you. These eyes will see miracles beyond all expectations, beyond your mind and your eyes. When my eyes replace yours, a whole new world will open up before you.

Appointed Time

This is what the Lord says ... Your baby was conceived in the Spirit by what you spoke, before she was conceived in the physical. She will come through the gate and follow the footsteps of Jesus. She will come through the gate just as you declare. Hebrew women are not like Egyptian women. They are vigorous and give birth before the midwives arrive. (Ex 1:19)

God is with your baby. The Lord says, I am in your belly with your baby. In my presence, she has fullness of joy. (Psalm 16:11) I will bring her through the birth canal at the appointed time. This will be a glorious, joyful occasion for you and your husband. My daughter, the Lord requests that the first Word the baby hears is the Word of the Lord. Just pray for it, and the Lord will silence everyone except those who speak the Word.

Phoenix

This is what the Lord says ... I rise like the phoenix within you. You hold onto the tips of my wings, and I carry you through all the discomfort, persecution, difficulties, and problems the enemy throws at you. Remember, you are climbing higher with me, as long as you are looking upwards at me. If you look down, I cannot bring you up. The phoenix rises from the ashes, and I give you beauty for ashes. You are being transformed on the Potter's wheel. And as long as you stay close to me, the finished vessel will be filled with peace, joy, wisdom, vision, all the fruits of the Spirit, and more. So, rest in me now. Do not strive, for I did not make you to work, but to reign.

Dressed in Glory

This is what the Lord says ... Just as your body is dressed with garments of fabric, your spirit is dressed in a garment of flesh. When someone's clothes are old and shabby, we say they look shabby. We know *they* aren't shabby, but it is the clothes. So too, when our garment of flesh is injured or torn, we should say it looks damaged or torn, but our spirit is not injured or torn. The Spirit I give my children is complete, whole, blessed, and pure. The blessings I have placed in your spirit will diffuse out of your spirit through your soul, body, and mind to demonstrate the glory of my Son, Jesus Christ—a body and mind at peace and in full health.

Path of Righteousness

This is what the Lord says ... Blessings from heaven are falling on my children. I shower them with gifts, the very gifts that fill places in their hearts, for it is the heart that matters. I mend the broken hearts with a love gift to heal each wound. As I heal the wounds, the heart opens like a flower, and the fragrance from the flowers is breathed in by everyone around them. It is the fragrance of heaven; an atmosphere is created, where my Son can stretch out his hand and bring you along the path I have for you. A path of righteousness where peace, joy, and freedom of abundance and the desires of your new mended heart will come to pass.

Your Journey - Step Number Three

I hope you have received the wholesome, soothing love of the Lord and have begun healing from past events. This is only the beginning. The more you engage with the Lord, the healing will continue until you are fully restored and free. Choose your favorite verse from this chapter. Recall in your memoir what events or spoken words hurt you deeply, and speak your favorite verse into those situations. Apply the love of the Lord lavishly into those wounds and observe the healing that occurs. It is a journey, so trust in the Lord that he is working on the inside before you see it on the outside.

Chapter 4

He Leads Me on the Right Path – The Faith Path

Psalm 23:2

"He guides me along the right paths
For His name's sake."

After I had given my life to God, I asked him to close the doors he didn't want me to go through and only open the door he did want me to go through. From that day onwards, at every juncture in my life, I have requested God to do this, and he has always led me to the right step along the path. I knew I could easily take a wrong turn. I have often diverted off the path but quickly realized that something wasn't right and called on the Lord, and his satellite navigation got me back on the right road.

The currency of the walk with the Lord is faith. But what is faith? Hebrews 11:1 states, "Now faith is confidence in what we hope for and assurance about what we do not see." So faith is dependent on hope and assurance. You already have faith! You hoped to hear from God through this book and trusted him enough to act on that hope by reading this book. Now apply that faith, hope, and trust, and the Lord will lead you in everything you do and say. Allow your faith to grow and move into all areas of your life. Faith requires perseverance and patience; if you are not abundant in these, ask the Lord to supply them.

Blueprint

This is what the Lord says ... I opened the eyes of the blind. I opened the ears of the deaf. I make strong, the weak. I find the lost. I heal the sick and mend the broken-hearted. There is nothing that I can't do for you, my children, whom I love with an everlasting love. When I gave my Son, Jesus, I gave my heart to you. You have my heart, and I long for your heart. I created the Garden of Eden so that we may fellowship together there.

But now you live in the world. You can bring the Garden of Eden into the world through me, and there we can fellowship together. I have laid out riches and treasures for you in the world that you may find them. They are not hidden from you, but hidden for you, that you and your children may have them forever. People search and search, work and work for treasures and riches.

However, the true treasure is living inside you, and I am the compass for where your riches, your treasures, are. The compass directs you on the path of my Son, Jesus. If you walk in the direction Jesus takes you, the treasure you will see, the riches you will have, blessings you will have. Blessings are already on your life. They are already attached to you. But they have not all manifested yet. Few walk the path, so many are lost from what belongs to them.

Therefore, I treasure each of you, my children, who walk on the path with my Son, Jesus. It blesses me so much to see you call out to me, speak my Word, walk with Jesus, learn from the Holy Spirit, and fulfill the plan that I have created you to have. My plan is for you to bless others, rejoice in the name of Jesus, and have everything fulfilled in your life that I have promised for you. This is the blueprint I have laid out for your path.

Dance with Me

This is what the Lord says ... You dance around me, but you don't dance with me. You have a heart full of desires and visions I have placed in you, some of which only you and I know of. When you delight in my Son, Jesus, I can give you all the desires of your heart. I have placed many gifts within you, which I will draw from you. Come and dance with me now that my arms may protect you. I will lead the dance, and you will not stumble, for I will place your foot on every step of the path. On this path, I will draw gift after gift out of your belly.

Heavenly Shoes

This is what the Lord says ... There is no other than I. You put your toe in the sand. I have put my imprint there before you. I am the shoe around your spiritual feet. For you do not have feet of clay, but feet from heaven. You do not plow the ground as others do, but your feet rest in me. They flow to the rhythm of the rivers of the Holy Spirit. There are no rocks in the rivers of living water. But if you take your feet out of my heavenly shoe, then rocks may find you. You are hidden in me and will walk very far with ease and comfort. I am here to protect you always.

Winds of Change

This is what the Lord says ... I see you through my eyes. I want you to see you through my eyes. I have given you my eyes. All you have to do is open those eyes, and you will see all I have created, designed, and placed around you. Your eyes will see through things, beyond the present, into the future. There will be winds of change. But these winds will blow away what I don't want and blow in what I do want. I am creating through you and for you all around you the environment in which you will flourish and develop like a garden coming to fruition with my fruits—the fruit of the Spirit.

Moving Forward Together

This is what the Lord says ... I am turning things around for you. Many have come against you, but you have stood firm. You are rooted in my Word. You do not sway with the world. You stand with me. I am going to push you forward very soon. And you will be exposed as you move forward. I move and step in next to you. I can only move through you. The greater freedom you give me in your life, the greater the power and the glory will be demonstrated. You are on the right path. Your feet are perfectly positioned, and your heart is mine. What more could I ask of a child? We will move forward. We will move forward together, and you will be astonished at what I will do through you.

Grace to Grace

This is what the Lord says ... The world is in chaos. The world is confused. You are so refined in your spirit, it stirs up the world around you. You're on the path with me. No one can stir you off it. You embrace the opportunity to grow in your faith. This gives me great joy, as I know I can stretch and stretch you. You are moving in my grace, going from Grace to Grace. You have your eye on me. You know where I want you to be. We are partners, a team moving together. Your faith can bring you all things, all places.

Currency of Faith

This is what the Lord says ... I have primed you for such a time as this. I have grown you up, though you are still growing. I am launching you into a new realm where you will see new things and hear me even more clearly. A step closer to me. I will reveal things to you unseen by everyone else. These unveilings will guide you on your path. You will have insider knowledge from me. It's like a new lighting system along the path, a more sophisticated one, so to speak. You will be in awe of what you see, but you will know it's me revealing it all to you. Faith is the currency by which you receive.

Stretch and Bend

This is what the Lord says ... I walk with you, and you walk with me. Sometimes I carry you, but you never carry me. I bless the ground you walk on; it is holy ground. I stretch you and bend you, and you do not resist. I stretch you and bend you even further. Yet you do not resist. I can take you anywhere as long as I continue to stretch and bend you.

Wait Patiently

This is what the Lord says ... Every day I walk with you, you are walking the path I have set out for you. You don't know where you are going, but you see the end goal. The path is not always easy, and many come against you. But you are resilient, and I have made you so. Everything you need for your journey, I will give you. I will either place it inside you or create the opportunity for you. You ask for so little, and you wait patiently for it. It will ALL come to you. You will see all the desires of your heart. Have no fear, no doubt for I am with you all the way.

Glory Upon Glory

This is what the Lord says ... There is no greater road than the road you are walking right now. You trust me, though you do not see me. You believe in my power and goodness, though I have not shown you. We are so close together, you and I, though you do not realize it. You have surrendered yourself to me and my will, just as my Son surrendered himself to me and my will. You are walking the walk with Jesus.

I am drawing the gifts out of you now. Soon, at the right time, you will see my glory, and you will send the glory back to me. I will bless you with glory upon glory, because you will continue to send the glory back to me and honor me. Just as the commandment says, "Honor your father and your mother," (Exodus 20:12) You honor your Father in heaven.

Growing Pains

This is what the Lord says ... You are in the eye of the storm and to move out of the storm you must go through the turbulence. Fear not, for I have made a path for you through the turbulence, and I am always with you. You will come through unscathed, promoted, strong, and mature. It is only a growth stage. It is only growing pains. You are growing into what I desire for you— and I am blessing you every day.

Darkness Retreats

This is what the Lord says ... Everything is moving, everything is changing. You are changing, and therefore, everything else is changing around you. The darkness cannot withstand the light. It has to retreat. As you move further and further on to where I want you to be, the darkness has to continue to retreat. Once established, the darkness will disappear. It will run, as you will have won that battle. As I move you on again, the battle will come to you again. Fear not, for I am leading you in it all. The war has already been won by my Son, Jesus.

Power Switch

This is what the Lord says ... Behold my hand, it is free to turn you in any direction. You have released yourself to me, and your flexibility will allow me to have a significant impact. Your hand is in my hand. I am always with you. I stand in front of you when you are being attacked. No one gets to you without going through me first. I permit those things to help you grow and develop that my power may be released through you. You are full of power, though I have not turned the switch on yet.

Written in Heaven

This is what the Lord says ... I write, you write. What is written in heaven is written on earth. My prophets have written heavenly words on earth. As my Son declared, "It is written ..." (Luke 4:4a) and so now you write for me and you will declare what is written.

Surrender Is Key

This is what the Lord says ... I will announce the right time for which events will unfold in your life. The clock is in my hand, and I set the alarm for events to occur. You will be prepared just as you have prepared for exams and interviews. Though the events will be spontaneous, you are ready and have the tools and gifts to respond to the task. Rest in me fully and let me step further, your surrender is key. Let my utterances come through your tongue, sight through your eyes, voice through your ears, and healing hands through your hands. Though you have surrendered your heart and life to me, now surrender your body, that I may minister through it like never before.

Road Less Traveled

This is what the Lord says ... I am raising you up, drawing you ever closer to me. I will give you signs and road marks as you walk the road with me. These are new road marks as you are on a new road with me. A road of discovery. And these road marks will be the treasures I reveal to you. You have walked a path without knowing the steps, yet holding on to my hand. This new road will be lit up with road markings. It will be clear to everyone around you that you are on a less-traveled road. But this road comes to me. As you walk this road, people will want to walk it too, and they will come onto it and follow the steps you have taken to come to me. For I shepherd you from here in heaven, and I shepherd them through you.

Solid Foundation

This is what the Lord says ... You're my child full of grace and promises. I've separated you out. You are not like everyone else, but a beacon of my light. I have carved out a difficult path for you, full of twists and bends. This strengthens your spiritual muscles. It will enable you to go into battle grounded in the Word. I see you now, for every challenge you come to my Word for guidance, strength, and comfort. I see you stand amid the world on my Word, while chaos and conflicts surround you. You are standing on the Word, standing on the shoulders of Jesus. Your foundation is solid. Nothing can move you from your perch unless you step off it.

Revelation

This is what the Lord says ... I see beyond all things, and I am taking you there. I'm stripping away the spiritual blindness that everyone has from your eyes. I will gradually unveil my vision to you. Once you receive that revelation, nothing will ever be the same again. When this happens, you will seek my counsel in everything (just as you do now) before revealing anything to anyone else. This is where I want you to fully operate in my realm and execute my plans for the world. You and I make a great team. We agree, and therefore it is established.

Faith Generated

This is what the Lord says ... I rise before you. I cleared the path and straightened it. Upon this path are treasures of gold, trunks and trunks of treasures of gold, and within each trunk, there is a gift. If you receive that gift, the treasure comes with it. Through it, I supply all your needs with abundance—no poverty or lack, no shade or darkness. There is only light, freedom, joy, and abundance of health, finance, and relationships.

As you grow in me, you come along the path. As you do, you receive each gift, and the abundance is released with it. I am healing all areas of your life, all areas of your heart, mind, and soul. As I pour my Word into you and you pour my Word back to me, this generates faith. Faith comes to receive and lay the gift on the path.

But your gift must be used wisely, for you can have a gift, but if it's not used wisely, the treasure will not manifest. The fruit of the gift is the treasure. You may collect gifts and treasures along the path, blessing you and all around you. Everyone will see the blessings in your life and your spirit. They will be eager to come onto the path with you, but only you can walk your path. They will have to go to Jesus and come onto the path that is laid out for them.

Walk the Straight Line

This is what the Lord says ... I walk a straight line. All those who walk this straight line are blessed. Those who leave the straight line are lost. But from the line, you will reach out to those lost and bring them to where they belong: the comfort of my company, my love, and my protection. You will not step off the line as you were established on it. For you have spoken it many, many times to secure yourself with me. You are my anchor out there. Those who attach themselves to you will attach themselves to me.

Unknown Territory

This is what the Lord says ... You are stepping into unknown territory. You are going where the eye cannot see, but you see in your heart. The storms are blowing, but you are in my strong tower. My shield of favor surrounds you. Little by little, I am unveiling the steps of your path. You've been so faithful to me. Treasures such as this new teaching gift are being released from your belly. Such treasures I have placed in you the day I knit you in your mother's womb. Guard every step you take, so that you do not step off the path I walk with you.

Lumps of Coal

This is what the Lord says ... You have been so faithful to me over many years while still in the darkness. Your faithfulness will change the lumps of coal that have rained down on your family into jewels. Throughout your family, there will be an explosion of light, and it will be all due to your faithfulness.

Unimaginable Treasures

This is what the Lord says ... I have created a world within you that you could not see. As you are coming further along the faith path, you are stepping into the revelation and beginning to see the treasures I've placed inside you. There is no hard toil in discovering this treasure, but a gentle, flowing stream of revelation which will grow to a river overflowing. Your time with me has been so precious that whenever you release part of yourself to me, I can move closer to you and open up another treasure.

The enemy may have stolen from you, but no longer. I will replace anything lost or stolen with a greater abundance. You will continue on the path with me until the enemy can no longer reach you and meddle in your life. You are the head, not the tail, (Deuteronomy 28:13) and no weapon forged against you will prosper. (Isaiah 54:17) I have unimaginable treasures within you, and this is only the beginning.

Light of Living Waters

This is what the Lord says ... The light of my Son, Jesus, has been switched on all around the world. Those who walked in darkness received Jesus, and the light was switched on in them. Those who received the Word and want to make Jesus Lord of their lives have a light on their path. Jesus lights up their path and guides each place they place their foot. The more you allow Jesus to be Lord of your life, the bigger, stronger, and brighter the light becomes. Eventually, the light overflows out of you, the light of living waters.

Love Bomb

This is what the Lord says ... I am creating in you a love bomb. This bomb will explode so big that it is not even in your imagination yet. When it is fully formed in your imagination, then I can release it. Every turn of the Potter's wheel brings you closer to the dream I have for your life. Eventually, the molding ends and the polishing begins. Until that time, stay close to me and trust me. For I am the Potter and am refining you all the time.

Faith Grows

This is what the Lord says ... I opened you up like a flower. You produce the fragrance of heaven. For you to flower, there must be a seed, water, nourishment, and patience. I provide all your needs, but I need you to cooperate with me and apply them. When you place a seed in the ground, you ensure it's watered and nourished, and you are patient. I make it grow. But when the seed goes into you, I give you living water. I give you the food. I supply all your needs. But your faith makes it grow and bloom into a beautiful flower.

Jesus Provider

This is what the Lord says ... I opened my heart, and out you came. You were created in my heart before I brought you forth and knitted you together in your mother's womb. My Son has laid out a path of peace, freedom, and joy, full of blessings for your life. Your brother, Jesus, gave all of himself that you might receive him and have victory in every circumstance you find yourself in. There is no person, no situation, no weapon that can have victory over you if you walk the path with Jesus. "So if the Son sets you free, you will be free indeed." (John 8:36)

Words of Yesterday

This is what the Lord says ... I take your hand, direct your path. You know where you're going, but you don't see every step on the journey. This journey is filled with gifts and desires of your heart. You have placed these gifts on the path, having declared them to be. I will not let my Word return to me empty (Isaiah 55:11) you sent it full of faith. Through your faith, I have placed them there, and now that your faith has brought you to a place on the path that you are ready to receive, you will see what you have spoken. The words of yesterday, you will walk on tomorrow.

Seasons

This is what the Lord says ... It is springtime all around. It is springtime in your life. The old dead branches have been cut away, and the shoots are coming through. You are beginning to blossom as the summertime of your spiritual growth truly comes as a new season. Summertime is followed by the harvest season. The fruit of the many years of plowing, planting, watering, endurance, and patience will have been worth it. When you step into the promised land of your spirit, the harvest will renew continually, as long as you stay on the path with Jesus and continue to declare my Word.

The Path Is Prepared

This is what the Lord says ... I am the answer—the answer to all your questions. I have answered them in my promises to you. You don't have to question whether I will do something. It is already done. All the paths have been prepared. It just takes you to walk it. Walk it without fear or hesitancy.

I am walking with you, for I am within you. And when you turn off the path to the right or left, I will quicken your spirit to redirect you back onto the path. Nothing will be lost, all promises fulfilled.

Foot Is Secure

This is what the Lord says ... I see the struggles in your life. Know that I am with you, in you, all around you. Do not grow weary, for I am growing you up on a sure-footed path. If I allowed you to run, you might fall. But every place you set your foot, I put it there. I've shown you the end from the beginning, yet the end is only the beginning.

My great plan for you is so big, your foot must always be secure in me. You have weathered many battles, but your armor is secure, and your faith has been tested. I will not allow you to be tested beyond what you can bear. (1 Corinthians 10:13) Though the devil tries to disrupt your home, family, and colleagues, you have stayed in peace and in my Son, Jesus. During the challenges that will come in the future, you will remain in peace and have compassion for those who come against you, for you know they are spiritually blind.

Palm of My hand

This is what the Lord says ... I elevate and I bring down. I am in control. I elevate my children, and I bring down their enemies. No one can stand against you. For I am standing with you, and I am in control. The whole of heaven is at your back, and though not one man may cover you, I cover you. The power and elevation that will come through you and to you, all comes from me. It is from my plan and my instruction. Know that you are in the palm of my hand, and I will not let you fall.

Your Journey – Step Number Four

Faith is the highest currency available. You can grow your faith. Romans 10:17 states, "Consequently, faith comes from hearing the message, and the message is heard through the Word about Christ." Faith is the key to receiving from the Lord. Meditate on scriptures regarding faith and observe how your hope and confidence in the Word will deepen and strengthen. Record your journey into the scriptures and how they have spoken to you. Review the questions in the Bonus gift and watch your faith grow.

Chapter 5

In the Presence of My Enemies – Always Leads Me in Victory

Psalm 23:5

"You prepare a table before me in the presence of my enemies."

Many years ago as a young Christian, I started to declare what God said about me. As I drove into work, I would speak 1 John 4:4 (KJV) in my own words … "I am a child of the living God and '… greater is he that is in [me], than he that is in the world." One day, a junior colleague made a minor mistake, and I assisted them in correcting it. A little while later, another colleague became involved and was verbally unpleasant, accusing me of making the mistake. (I knew I wasn't on this person's favorites list!)

As they vigorously expressed their opinion, I reverted quietly in my mind to 1 John 4:4 and declared to myself, *I am a child of the living God.* When the person finished what they were saying, I calmly explained what had happened. The person left the room to return a few minutes later and admitted the junior colleague made the mistake but again was verbally very unpleasant.

They left the room, and I said, "God, what is happening?" The person came back a third time, but this time apologized profusely. Although shaken, I said, "It's not a problem, we can forget about it now." I was stunned!! I knew God had spoken to this person and put it in their heart to come back and apologize to me. It was incredible!!

An even more incredible thing happened a few days later. I was walking by this person, and they called me aside and asked me, "Do you really forgive me?" I responded, "Yes, of course, it has been forgotten, so don't worry about it."

The Lord began to show me that wounded people operate from a wounded place. I had empathy for this person before this incident occurred. I had not responded in the flesh but in the spirit, and the Lord Jesus took up the mantle to defend my Father's honor in protecting his child. Thinking back on it now makes me cry with joy.

Ephesians 6:12 reads, "For our struggle is not against flesh and blood, but against the rulers, against the authorities, against the powers of this dark world and against the spiritual forces of evil in the heavenly realms."

If you respond from your emotions, then the Lord cannot intervene. We must respond in the spirit with the Word of God, and Jesus will rescue us.

The Father does not just remove us from difficult circumstances, but he provides for us in those hard places. He gives us Jesus through whom we have the victory, whatever the situation.

2 Corinthians 2:14, "But thanks be to God, who always leads us as captives in Christ's triumphal procession and uses us to spread the aroma of the knowledge of him everywhere."

We can easily become impatient while waiting for victory. But we are guaranteed the victory if we can stand in the midst of the battle and wait patiently on the Lord. The following verses describe how we can stand in the battle and emerge victorious. As the Lord says in our journey through the valley of darkness, even though we may be surrounded by enemies, he prepares a table for us, and on that table is the bread of life.

In John 6:35, it states, "Then Jesus declared, 'I am the bread of life. Whoever comes to me will never go hungry, and whoever believes in me will never be thirsty.'"

Stand Firm

This is what the Lord says ... I have knitted you in your mother's womb. (Psalm 139:13) I have walked with you through all the years you were growing up. I have seen you grow into a wonderful wife and mother. Through every step I have been there, and I am still here. I will never leave you nor forsake you. (Hebrews 13:5) Do not be afraid or discouraged because of this vast army. For the battle is not yours, but [mine.] (2 Chronicles 20:15b) You will not have to fight this battle. Take up your position, stand firm, and see the deliverance the Lord will give you. Do not be afraid. Do not be discouraged. Go out to face them tomorrow. And the Lord will be with you. (2 Chronicles 20:17) Cast your cares on to [me] because [I] care for you. (1 Peter 5:7)

Warrior by Nature

This is what the Lord says ... My child, you are a warrior by nature. I put in you the heart of a warrior that is in me. I have given you great gifts and abilities, and you have been a great steward of these gifts and abilities and have achieved much. There is a hunger in your heart that drives you to succeed, but that hunger is not a need to succeed but a hunger for me. Move closer to me now, my beautiful child, for I am eager to teach and show you more. You are a warrior in the physical world, but I want to make you a warrior in the spiritual world. When you bring my ability into every situation, you will see things beyond where your imagination can take you now. Move closer to me, my dear child.

Strong Tower

This is what the Lord says ... Every day, I look to you as you look to me. I see what is all around you. I see your enemies. I have a protective shield around you that cannot be penetrated. You are above all the arrows that the enemy sends your way. You're in my tower, protected. Relax where you are—fear not the how and when for only I know the how and the when. You just know my Word is true, and that will carry you through.

Success After Success

This is what the Lord says ... Anytime I am looking to you, I am looking to me. I have placed myself in you. When I call on you, I call on myself within you. I don't call on you, for you are only a part within me. Nobody asks an arm to do something, but it asks the body. I am the body within you. If the arm tries to do something without the body, it will fail.

Because you are the arm of my body you cannot do this without me, as you will not succeed. You are part of me now. So let me carry you in all that you do, and there will be a straight line of success after success—no defeat when I am with you.

Front-line Warrior

This is what the Lord says ... I keep you close at all times, and you stay close to me. My heart is full of joy for you. Walk the path with my Son, Jesus. You speak the words from my lips. I have put my heart inside you, a heart for the people who are broken and wounded. You are my front-line warrior. We have fought many battles together, but victory is always yours in Christ Jesus.

Armor of God

This is what the Lord says ... You, my child, are made in my image and likeness. You are the light, and the darkness reacts to the light. It is powerless. You are a laser light, and you are laser focused, on my plan for you. You are all powerful because I am in you. Stand firm and in peace, and all the storms surrounding you will pass away. There is no storm you cannot withstand. You are all-powerful. There can be no mistake when you consult me on everything you do and say.

Learn to rest in the midst of the storms, and your strength will not be depleted but will grow. In the past, the enemy has sent single storms which you weathered. Now he has to send many storms at once because you were getting stronger and stronger and resting in me more and more. The devil is running out of empty weapons to threaten you with. You have all the armor you will ever need. Continue to use them, and I will enforce them. Remember, you always have the victory in Jesus.

Sharp Sword

This is what the Lord says ... My hands are molding you. I am molding and refining the finest details, for you will be the sharpest sword I can make. You have allowed me to harness your tongue, removing the thoughts and the words the world has put in you. Now you are about to think my thoughts and speak my words. When you speak the words of my lips, the sword will be so sharp that nothing can stand that you command to fall, and nothing can fall that you command to stand. I will wrap my word around situations, and my breath will be on those words. The breath of creation, creating what is in my heart. I give you the desires of your heart, and you give me the desires of my heart.

Victory Words

This is what the Lord says ... You are a blessing unto me. As long as you speak victory, victory will be yours. Victory will make the way. It will be all around you. You won't be able to fail in anything, because my hand will turn to victory. I will guide you unto paths of victory. Never fear, whatever the situation, victory will prevail. There is no cost to you. All you have to do is say it.

You have given me a wonderful home within you. You make me feel welcome, always engaging with me and concerned about what I want. It doesn't compare to what I will do for you. I am stretching bigger and bigger within you. The more you surrender to me, the bigger I become and the more powerful I am through you. I have longed for many years for a daughter like you. Know I have you in the palm of my hand

and come with you everywhere you go. You have blessed me, but I will bless you beyond all expectations and dreams you could ever have. It will be a path of success after success—victory after victory. No struggle, just words.

Spine of Steel

This is what the Lord says ... I have anointed you, and no one else, for this position, for this purpose. And no one can take it off you unless you give it away as Adam did. Do not be tricked. You know the truth. I have set the vision in your heart for freedom from illness and disease for my children. You are so close now, and the enemy is emptying all artillery on you in his last attempt to take you down.

But though you have a crooked spine physically, spiritually, you have a spine of straight steel. You have built this yourself with the words of your mouth. You have created the pathway on which you walk, and you walk with dignity and honor. And the honor you give to me. The enemy's resources are disappearing rapidly, as they can only target the soul, the mind, the will, the emotions, and the body. As I release you from these worldly ties, your mind, will, and emotions move into the spiritual realm where I operate from. Enjoy the peace and joy of Jesus as you enter the spiritual realm, freeing yourself of worldly things. And there I can dress you in the finest that the spiritual realm has to offer you.

Walk Securely

This is what the Lord says ... I stand beside you in your battles. I walk with you through the darkness. I watch over you night and day, watching you sleep and breathe. For it is my breath that I have given you, the breath of life, and no one can take it away. Everywhere you go, everything you do, I am there to protect and guide you. In my presence, there is fullness of joy. Therefore, you should always be full of joy. But the devil comes to steal. Though you see the fruit of your faithfulness to me coming upon your family, deep in your heart, you feel insecure and unsure. Don't let doubt creep in when it comes knocking on the door of your heart. Say joy lives here, for the Lord lives in me. The devil will flee from those who walk with integrity, they walk securely. (Proverbs 10:9)

Rest Is a Weapon

This is what the Lord says ... Knowing you as I do, I see the light of me inside you. Fear not, for I have equipped you for all things. Rest in me continuously, and that will be your greatest weapon. For when you rest in me, you allow me to operate through you. All the declarations you have made, I can then execute. There is nothing I ask of you more than to surrender your heart to me. And you've done this. Rest and see the glory of God prevail in your life. It is something to behold.

The God Team

This is what the Lord says ... I go before you in everything. I go before you in your family, leisure, and job. I go before you as you enter into this new adventure. Know that you are not alone but blessed. You turn right, I turn right. You turn left, I turn left. There is no distance between us. I am as close to you as anyone could be. We are a team as we advance. When you go to present (in front of people) in the future, we go to present. Though the task may seem overwhelming, it is already established. All you have to do is put words on it, and it will be executed. The benefits will be enormous beyond what you can see now.

Army Is Ready

This is what the Lord says ... I am making changes in society—out with the old and in with the new. I will make changes across all areas of culture and life. I am moving out the old and bringing in my people. My people have sat with me in the quiet, soaked in my presence, received the Word, and groaned in the spirit. I have my people in all walks of life ready to spread my message and overcome the enemy's plots. My army is silent at the moment, but it has been prepared. It is ready to proceed at my command. Be assured, I have not forgotten. I have seen everything. I AM in control.

Perseverance in Battle

This is what the Lord says ... I am here for you to rest. And I am the rest into which you hide and feel safe. I am the strong hand that protects you. I am the voice that directs you and all around you, diverting good to you and evil away. I am the power behind your salvation and your eternal life. Your time on Earth is fleeting, but your time in heaven will be everlasting—such joy when you rest your head on heaven's pillow.

For now, you are on duty. You are my soldier, drawing the battle lines over which the enemy cannot cross. The battle lines you have drawn for this situation are the blueprint for all the battle lines you will draw in the future. To stand at the first battle is the most difficult, as the enemy will do everything to force you to concede. Then forever after, he will know you will always consider conceding. Stand strong now, and the enemy will know your strength and will retreat. The enemy will prolong the battle to wear you down, but perseverance is yours in every situation. I have filled you with my strength and perseverance, for you will do great things for me.

Enemy Is Weary

This is what the Lord says ... You are my light in the world. You are always switched on. You don't take your eyes off me, and I don't take my eyes off you, for you are the apple of my eye. When I look at you, I see my glory all around you. This is why the enemy comes to battle with you. But he is becoming weary, for he has tried everything and everyone. But you grow stronger and more peaceful than before. You are the image of me. You talk like me. You walk like me. Now you are entering another place where gifts will come pouring out of you, rivers of living water. And these waters are filled with gifts. Gifts that will bless you and many people.

Victory Through Our Lord Jesus Christ

This is what the Lord says ... You are my child, in whom I am well pleased. A warrior who steps into the darkness to bring the light, to bring hope to the lost and freedom to the captives. I have placed armor on you so strong that no man can take you down. Every day, you put that armor on and go forth ...

Do not be afraid or discouraged because of this vast army. For the battle is not yours, but [mine]. (2 Chronicles 20:15) For the struggle is not against flesh and blood, but against the rulers, against the authorities, against the powers of this dark world and against the spiritual forces of evil and the heavenly realms. Therefore, put on the full armor of God so that when the day of evil comes, you may be able to stand your ground, and after you have done everything, to stand. (Ephesians 6:12-13) Do not be afraid: do not be discouraged. Go out to face them tomorrow, and [I] will be with you. (2 Chronicles 20:17b) It is for freedom that Christ has set you free. Stand firm then and do not let yourselves be burdened again by a yoke of slavery. (Galatians 5:1) I give you victory through our Lord Jesus Christ. (1 Corinthians 15:57b)

Victory Never Leaves You

This is what the Lord says ... I have rescued you from the pit, the fires of hell. You are hidden in me. My favor surrounds you as a shield. I surround you. I am above you, below you, in front of you, and behind you. No weapon forged against you can prosper. You are the apple of my eye; my eye is always on you. My armor is upon you. Any weapon thrown at you is thrown at me. You don't have to defend me. Just stand, I will move the players in the game. Victory is always with you. Victory never leaves you or forsakes you.

My Hand on Your Life

This is what the Lord says ... I brought you to this place because you submitted yourself to me. You've allowed me to put my hand into your life and turn you anyway that pleases me. You are so obedient and disciplined, though many storms surround you to intimidate and frighten you. You are in my strong tower. You will not be moved. You are progressing to where I want you to be. The enemy reacts to you, but you don't react. Very soon, you will be unveiled, and the glory of God will shine through you.

Your Journey - Step Number Five

Victory is available for all areas of your life. However, the timing is in God's hands. He is faithful, and we have to be faithful in return. Recognize the battles in your life, health, finances, family, whatever they are—there is a victory waiting to be fulfilled. Identify which verse above applies explicitly to each battle described. Continue recording your personal memoir, the day you declared victory, and when it comes to pass. You will see that the victory comes at the ordained time.

Chapter 6

Anoint My Head With Oil – Unveiling My Purpose

Psalm 23:5

"You anoint my head with oil."

It has been ten years since I first encountered the Holy Spirit. I believe it was during this first encounter that the Holy Spirit anointed me for a great purpose. He told me I would have a publishing business called Holy Spirit Books. As a scientist, I rarely read anything besides science books, so I knew this wasn't my idea! It had to be God! I wanted to step out in faith, so I registered "Holy Spirit Books" as a business name in 2015. I didn't share this with anyone, I kept it private between God and me. I didn't understand this anointing, and I knew other people definitely wouldn't understand it. Therefore, I didn't want to lose confidence and be discouraged by what others would say. I knew God would bring it to pass if it was truly what he had planned for me.

You may not know the anointing God has planned for you. It may be demonstrated within your family or current workplace, or he may take you into another environment before he reveals it to you. But know that in Psalm 23, he first restores your soul, guides you along the right path, comforts you, and if you call on his Word in times of trouble, he is with you. Then he anoints your head with oil. He will reveal his plans to you.

Jeremiah 29:11 reads, "'For I know the plans I have for you,' declares the Lord, 'plans to prosper you and not to harm you, plans to give you hope and a future.'"

New Anointing

This is what the Lord says ... I'm taking you to another level. Not everyone can go with you. I have placed people along your path who will teach and encourage you to grow further. When you leave primary school, you no longer need teachers from the primary level. You are moving up. There is still so much growth ahead, but you are diligent in your spiritual life. You seek me constantly, and in doing this, you grow.

I am changing things; you will no longer be the follower but the leader, and people will follow you. They won't know where they are going, but you are guiding them to me. They see me in you, which is why they follow. I bless your days ahead with a new anointing of leadership. Everyone will notice that something is different about you, though they won't know what it is. It is me!

Separated but Inseparable

This is what the Lord says ... I rise within you. I am the power within you. Without me, you have no power. When you see me release my power through you, you will know the ability within you. Now you believe it is there because I tell you, soon you will believe it is there because you will see it. I am bound in you, and you are bound in me. We are inseparable now. I am taking off the scales you have leaned on. Leaned on for protection. I will be your only true protection. Lean on me.

I am taking you into a new realm—a whole new level of revelation. You will see every step in the spirit and will take every step with me. I am faithful to you. But you are also faithful to me. Never once have you turned away from me, rejected me, or doubted the promises and desires I have placed in you. That was why you were named Fidelma, which means Faith. I called you, as you would be. You have waited long, through great endurance, for my will to be fulfilled in your life. Soon, the girl who has been separated, rejected, and mocked will be clothed in my glory. And they will see you have been separated out for me, to be with me.

Anointed Words

This is what the Lord says ... I raise you up, as I do so, you come into an elevated position of protection. The greater you surrender, the more I, in my armor, can surround and protect you. You are deep in me now. The position I have put you in is creating shock waves throughout the spiritual and physical world every time you write. Though you may choose the words, each word is marked with my anointing, and it penetrates the heart.

You don't see what is happening around you, but you are creating earthquakes. There is shifting going on in high places because of the words you speak, just as Moses said the same words over and over to Pharaoh. You just keep saying what you are saying while everything around you is changing. You will be shocked when I reveal the impact of your words that you speak to me privately, and the words you speak openly will soon be revealed.

Rivers of Living Water

This is what the Lord says ... I will turn the king's heart towards you. I will turn it, says the Lord. It may not look like it will happen, but I can turn it any way I want. When his heart turns, then all the hearts will turn. Rivers of living waters will flow out of you upon them. They will be soaked in the Holy Spirit, and from the top, the rivers of living water will flow down onto the people, transforming all who receive it. The rivers of living waters don't flow up. They can't flow from where you are. But when I take you to the top, then the rivers will flow.

Hearts and Eyes

This is what the Lord says ...I see your eyes; I see your heart. I see me in your heart. Through your eyes, you will see into the hearts of others. You will know their thoughts and desires. You will see their motivation and be able to mold and direct them to me. When they see you, they will see me through you. Then their eyes will be open. Eyes become open when the heart is right with me. Eyes and hearts. Hearts and eyes.

Purpose

This is what the Lord says ... Every time you come to me, I respond. You don't always see that I have responded but know I have. I have watched you grow and develop spiritually, knowing your life has a great purpose. You will be like a magnet to people. They will see me through you and come to me through you. All you have to do is rest in me and follow my instructions when I give them. You will do this, and all the world will see me through you. At last, a child of mine will fulfill their purpose.

Fragrance of Heaven

This is what the Lord says ... I'm about to bring my flower into bloom. The petals are about to spring open to reveal the heart I have put in you, and the world will experience the fragrance of heaven. I've spent many years molding and refining you. You've been patient and submitted your soul to my Potter's hand. For the fruit of your spirit will feed the hungry, and you will direct them to the everlasting wine.

Flower of Hope

This is what the Lord says ... I open you up like a flower, a fragrant flower of hope. The fragrance from heaven carries hope to the lost, wounded, and broken people. When they smell hope, their hearts will open, and they will come. They will come because I call them. You don't have to call them. I will call them through you.

Torch

This is what the Lord says ... My light shines so brightly out of you. You are a torch to those in the dark. As you direct your torch to me, my lost children come to me. Your torch is getting brighter and brighter, going from a torch to a lighthouse that can light up a whole coastline. Your light doesn't just guide them to me, but it feeds them too. Once they taste the light, they realize they have a hunger for me. I rejoice that the sacrifice my Son, Jesus, gave is rewarded with the return of his brothers and sisters into the kingdom.

Water into Wine

This is what the Lord says ... I see you and me as one. All that is in me is in you. I am teaching you, and you are learning. Yes, turning water into wine is a gift I have placed in you. It is not your time yet, but it is coming.

Unveiling

This is what the Lord says ... I am doing a new thing. I will walk you through it. I will guide you every step of the way. I am establishing an environment in which you will thrive, where you will deliver my message. I am moving people out and moving others in. Fear not, for it is all in my hands. Just stand still with me and watch me move things all around you as I did in the past. When the movements are complete, then and only then will the time come to unveil you and you unveil me.

Love Bomb

This is what the Lord says ... I love you. I love you with an everlasting love. You will be my love bomb. I will pour my love into you, and you will pour it onto others, onto the sick, the lost, the bereaved. Everyone you meet will be poured upon with love. Even if they don't want it, you won't be able to help yourself. The love will be so powerful. People will flee from it due to its power, but many will run to it. Many, many, many people will sit and soak up my love when they are in your presence. You will be my love bomb.

Bus Stop

This is what the Lord says ... When you walk with me, I walk with you. When you look in the spirit, you look through my eyes. When you lay hands on people, they will be my hands. I nurture you to become like me. I mold you and refine you. Your ears will hear me and nothing else. You will hear me so clearly. The task I have put on your life is enormous. But it is not your task, it is mine. You are my tool, pliable and flexible in my hands.

Through you, I am free to connect with my children to call them to me, so eventually they will all be seated with me in heavenly places. You are like a bus collecting my children and dropping them off to me in heaven. I have many fleets of buses, but many are not in operation. They are idle. But you bring joy to heaven as you operate your bus service. I change the route frequently, but you follow my directions precisely.

Teary Eyed

This is what the Lord says ... I created you for great things, for a great purpose. For you have my Son, Jesus, inside you. Tears fill my eyes every time you surrender to me and when I count another soul saved. You give me all of yourself to mold and refine. Few come to me like that. The purpose of your life is so big that it will change the world. Thousands will be saved. People won't be able to deny me when they see the road you walk, and you will declare it is Jesus who walks with you.

Doorpost

This is what the Lord says ... I see you; I hear you, I am with you. I respond to you. I'm generous to you. I ask you to do things, and you do them. I will continue to ask, and you will continue to do things. You do not always know or understand my plan for you, but you come anyway, trusting me. Through that trust, I can help many people and bless you. I am joyful to step into people's lives through you. They open the door and invite me in.

You are like the doorpost. You have created the frame through which I walk. I create the spiritual path you walk on, but you create the doorpost through which I step. There will be many, many doorposts created, and I will step through all of them because my children are crying out to me but don't know how to reach me. I will reach them through you, and we will be together in heaven.

You Are a Powerhouse.

This is what the Lord says ... I will tie up demons because of you. I will free my children. I will rebuke the devil through you. They (demons) will run when they see you coming. They know you know who you are. They know you have me, the almighty, powerful one. They see that power flows through you, even from a distance, without opening your mouth. You are my powerhouse. You are the generator that directs the power. There will be profound changes when I release my power through you. You won't know what is happening at first, but you will learn that when you have learned to release my power, extraordinary things, never seen before, will happen. And you will turn all the glory over to me.

Spotlight

This is what the Lord says ... You have just stepped into the spotlight. But you are the spotlight. You are the torch, mighty and strong, shining to show my people the way to me. Many turn away from the light and hide in the darkness. But now my light is going to shine everywhere. There will be nowhere for them to hide. I am looking straight at them, and they will know my eyes see them.

Stepping out

This is what the Lord says ... I see you growing in me and I in you. You trust me, and I trust you. We have an unbreakable bond now. I will ask you to step out, and you will do it, knowing I am stepping with you. I invite you to starve yourself of the world, and you will do it. Generous and kind, you will grow. Always looking to me, asking me which way to go. We are on the same path. If only others would join us on that path. I have my people all around you, though they have not stepped out yet. I will ask them to step out, and then you will see them surrounding you, supporting you. Generous and kind, all the time you are growing, I bless you with a blessing not given since Abraham because you receive it. Rest in me.

Masterpiece

This is what the Lord says ... "I know the plans I have for you. Plans to prosper you and not to harm you. Plans to give you hope in the future." (Jeremiah 29:11) You are now about to enter the future I have created through you. You will ebb and flow with me. You will see highs and lows, but I will always be with you. The darkness may surround you, but I cover all of you in light. I am working on a great thing in you, a masterpiece that the world will be in awe of.

I have placed many, many masterpieces within so many people, but they will not allow my hands to mold and develop them, and so they are never brought into the light display. You will teach them that they are safe with me. By giving me all the glory that comes to you, they will know that I can do with them what I am doing with you. You will be a leader to many people you will never meet, but they will hear me through you and follow you to reach me.

Your Journey - Step Number Six

The anointing God has planned for you is unique to you, and no one can carry out the plans he has for your life except you. You are special to the Father, and he has made special plans for you. The anointing mantle, which he will place on you, will be a mantle shared with Jesus. For he will walk with you under this mantle as your purpose is expressed. If the Lord has already revealed to you your purpose, but it seems overwhelming, just allow the Lord to grow you up into that purpose, and at the ordained time, it will be fulfilled. Continue recording your journey with the Lord by pressing into scripture around the anointing of Biblical characters and reviewing the questions in the Bonus gift.

Chapter 7

My Cup Overflows – Abundance

Psalm 23:5

"My cup overflows."

The overflowing cup of peace is probably the greatest blessing I have received from the Lord. When I first encountered the Holy Spirit, he told me I worried too much and not to worry any longer. I didn't know how not to worry! But, as I searched the scriptures, I found Jesus is described in Isaiah 9:6b as the "Prince of Peace."

As I sought out Jesus, I came across a very powerful scripture. Philippians 4:7 says, "And the peace of God, which transcends all understanding, will guard your hearts and your minds in Christ Jesus."

As I meditated on this scripture and declared it over my life, the peace of heaven penetrated all areas of my life. I don't worry about anything anymore. The Lord is now in control and oversees everything in my life, and I just stay in peace.

When we think of abundance, we immediately think of wealth in terms of financial wealth. However, the Father has a different approach to abundance:

"Peace I leave with you; my peace I give you. I do not give to you as the world gives. Do not let your hearts be troubled and do not be afraid." (John 14:27)

"But seek first his kingdom and his righteousness, and all these things will be given to you as well." (Matthew 6:33)

The Father wants to give us abundance on the inside before we see abundance on the outside.

The Heart, The Seed

This is what the Lord says ... I placed a seed inside the flesh of an apple, just as I placed a heart inside the flesh of your body. When the seed of the apple is in the right environment and has all it needs, a miracle happens. It becomes a shoot, eventually a tree with a harvest of thousands of apples, year after year, faithfully. Your heart, the seed I have placed in you, can do the same thing when in the right environment. It begins to shoot out a gentle spray of love. This becomes a little stream of love, eventually becoming a river of love, overflowing from you. Just like the seed is the source that produces the apples that feed thousands of people's bodies, your heart is the source that produces the love that feeds thousands of people's spirits.

Fruit will come

This is what the Lord says ... I cherish you, my child. I hear the cries of your heart, your eagerness to come into my presence. I am always here. Your vulnerability gives me the opportunity to embrace you. Your questions allow me to answer you, though you are looking around you all the time for the evidence of me and answered prayer. You must look inside yourself, for there is the evidence—the workmanship I am doing within you. Don't be disillusioned, for it is out of my work that the blessings will come into view. For I have cut away the unwanted dead branches so the living branches can flourish and produce fruit. Though it takes time, the fruit will come.

Harvest is Great

This is what the Lord says ... I created you inside and out. I know every part of my creation. I know what my hands have made and what an impostor is. I have molded you as a baby in your mother's womb. And I continue to mold you in the bosom of my spirit. Growth takes time, but the harvest is great. So few have the tenacity and patience to endure the walk with my Son, Jesus. But you walk step by step with him on the path I have laid out for you. Brother and sister walking on the path of my will. The treasures I have for you are so great that your mind cannot yet comprehend. I must bring you to a place where your mind can receive all the things before you see them.

Pulse of my Beating Heart

This is what the Lord says ... I love you, my child, with an everlasting love. You don't realize the extent of my love. I bring it all around you. I am showing you every day. You don't realize how present I am in your life. I am watching you, guiding you, protecting you all the time. I don't take my eye off you. I never sleep. You will step out soon, and I will step out with you. Then you will see me and the power of my love for you. You will feel the pulse of my beating heart for you. Every move you make, I will move with you. I trust in every move you make as you seek me and my counsel for every move you make. Rest in me, all is well.

Love Bubble

This is what the Lord says ... I read your mind. I see your thoughts. I know what you think and how you think. Because you have my Word in you, you think like me, though you do not know my ways. You know my thoughts because my thoughts are your thoughts now. So, fear not what is to come. I am so close to you, though you cannot see it. I am all around you. My shadow covers you, my arms around you and my love envelops you. You are in a love bubble with me, and it is a Teflon bubble. Nothing can get through it.

Wings of Success

This is what the Lord says ... I never see failure. I only see success. You're on the wings of success. You are secure in me and can never fail. I am bringing you a new way of life. The life you've always dreamed of. It is about to be unveiled. Maturity and time have come together. It will be all and more than you've ever dreamed or expected. It will be an anointed family, not since Jesus, Mary, and Joseph has such an anointing been placed on a family. All things will come together for your good. The miracles and dreams that your anointing will draw out have never been seen before on the earth. I AM doing a new thing.

Fragrance of Heaven

This is what the Lord says ... Everything you have, I give to you. I give you the things you do not see; the blessings of heaven are on your spirit. I have placed them there expecting you to see them unveiled like a flower and bloom, layer after layer. You are the blessing. And as you walk with me, you are unveiled, layer by layer, until you blossom and your full beauty is visible to all, and you emit the fragrance of heaven.

Promised Gifts

This is what the Lord says ... Everything I do is for the love of my children. I created a garden that I might visit with them. I created a heaven where they might live with me. My heart aches to protect and cherish my children, but many believe I am a God of cruelty rather than a God of love. The devil deceived those who should believe, for those who believe all heaven is open to them, send your servant-faith to heaven to pull down the promised gifts I have for you here. There are gifts assigned to be delivered to you. Don't let time pass without receiving them.

Gardener's Hands

This is what the Lord says ... I gave you a pair of creative hands so that you may create things for me. I gave you knowledge in your heart and tenderness in your fingers that you may grow plants for me. I gave you a nose so that you would recognize the perfume of every flower. I have given you a vision that you will create a Garden of Eden for me so that we can walk, talk, and laugh together. And I can teach you all I know. For I have given you my very own gardener's hands.

Endless Resources

This is what the Lord says ... I am the power, glory, and source of all your strength and joy. Draw out of me, for I have endless resources from which I can supply you. Whatever you need, you can receive from me. You have already received it, but it must be released. Turn the switch on with the release of the Word, and the power and resources become activated in your life.

Abundance of Promises

This is what the Lord says ... I placed the dreams in you. These are my dreams for you. I have created heaven on earth all around you. The house, the husband, and the animals are all for you. You are learning to draw it out of the wells of your belly. Slowly but surely, you are seeing what I have provided in abundance for you. As you step deeper into faith, deeper into me, you will see the things you have spoken for years come to pass again and again. For just as Elijah spoke my Words, the abundance of rain came. So too, you have spoken my Words. And the abundance of promises revealed will fall on you. Just as you say it, and it will be done.

Out of Your Belly

This is what the Lord says ... I write everything you say in my book. You write everything I say in your book. We are letter writers or pen pals. Every day, I have something special to say to you that I want you to write down. Your spiritual wells are full of my Word, they are overflowing into your physical life through your mind, body, and soul. You step closer and closer to me all the time. The time is near for those living waters to continually flow out of your belly. You won't be able to speak anything other than what I say to you. You are my spokeswoman, and the world will hear what I have to say. I am well pleased with you, my loyal and faithful daughter.

Full Bloom

This is what the Lord says ... You are my flower, and I am opening your petals one by one until you are in full bloom. You have been rooted in me for many years, but you could not push through the earth on your own. Then the Holy Spirit came and whispered into your heart. And you sprang up with joy. You have brought joy to my heart to see you full of my joy. When you are in full bloom, the glory of God will be so evident that your flower will spread and become a garden. A garden where my children can fellowship once again with me through you.

Eternal Clock

This is what the Lord says ... Open up your heart now, that I may place a love gift within. I have created for you a most loving husband. He is generous and kind, full of the fruit of the Spirit. I have molded him on the Potter's wheel for many years, just as I have molded and sculpted you. You are a pair who are about to come together. When that happens Heaven will rejoice, for my will, will be done in both of your lives. A promise fulfilled for both of you.

You will go forth as one full of love, joy, and strength. Every time you two come to agreement, I will do it because you have waited on me for such a long time. You have not watched the earthly clock but the eternal clock. For you will be like Adam and Eve were once in the garden with me, one in spirit with me. You will fulfill the desire of my heart to have my family close around me again.

New Seeds of Desire

This is what the Lord says ... I have planted a new seed for the love of music. The words I give you will be the expression of me through the music, and you will compose the melody, the song of heaven. I have taken you from scientist to poet, publisher, and I will take you to music composer, and on and on … I will take you, for I am an unlimited, all-powerful, all-skillful God.

As you surrender to me and release your worldly desires, I step right in and begin to create the circumstances in which you will see your spiritual desire. These desires I have placed in you. Just as my Son Leonardo da Vinci was poet, artist, engineer, scientist, you too will operate in multiple gifts, and I will add no toil to it. All my children have this potential, but they can only be fulfilled through my Son, Jesus.

Treasures

This is what the Lord says ... Everywhere you stand, I stand. You stand amid your enemies, your cup overflows. I am doing a new thing. I am taking away the old to make room for the new. A new family for you. There is pain in letting go of the old, but there is joy in the new. "Crying may last for a night, but joy cometh in the morning." (Psalm 30:5b) You have seen your path, but now you will see it more clearly. I am moving you on, moving you up. You are already established. It cannot be denied. Jesus always has the victory. I will show you new things, magnificent things. You and everyone around you will be in awe. Treasures just for you and your new family. Treasures in abundance.

Special Gifts

This is what the Lord says ... I am raising you up to a new position. It is not a position that already exists. It is being created for you for the special gifts I have put inside of you. You will exercise these gifts to your astonishment and the astonishment of all those around you. The Holy Spirit will just flow through you, and you will allow it to happen. You will be obedient in all requests, though you do not always understand. The people around you will know the Lord is with you, and they will seek my wisdom through you. You have surrendered yourself to me many times and will continue to do so. As we walk together, you and I, I can do more and more through you, and my presence on the earth will be felt once again. The people will know that I am the Lord, and they will know you are with me.

A Different Life Now

This is what the Lord says ... I have created an enterprise for you, one that will contain many facets and gifts I have and will give you. It will unveil you, and in doing so, unveil me. You will be noticed, but you will carry my name everywhere. As you do, doors will be opened, opportunities will come from nowhere, totally unexpected. It will be a magnificent display of my love and my power. People will be drawn to you because of my glory shining through you. You will never leave me, and I will never leave you. We are one now and forever. I bless everything you do everywhere you go. Blessings surround you. You see what I am doing in your life. You see your life before, full of struggle and disappointment. You have a different life now, full of success and blessings. As you rest, my grace carries you on.

Sweet Notes of the Heart

This is what the Lord says ... I've grown you up to the place where you are today. Tomorrow, I will grow you up further, and the next day and the day after that, as long as you keep surrendering to me, I can continue to stretch and mold you. You are still on the Potter's wheel. But you are where I want you to be, and you will be an instrument I can use. However, I will continue to refine you so that the music from you gets sweeter and sweeter, and those notes penetrate straight through to the hungry hearts of my lost children. There is no limit to where I can take you, as long as you continue to surrender to me.

Tears of Gold

This is what the Lord says ... Through it all, you depended on me. Through all the tears, all the pain. I have turned every tear into gold and placed it back in your heart, so nothing was lost. Your heart is now filled with gold. The tears have been replaced by gold. And you are about to overflow like a gold chalice. You have already touched so many people, but you are now coming into a whole new level.

Your light is undimmable. It's just getting brighter and brighter. There is no end to the people you are going to touch. You are still on the Potter's wheel, and you will do great things for me. Your purpose is secure in me. Protected by me. "No weapon forged against you can prosper." (Isaiah 54:17) "You give me the desire of my heart," (Psalm 37:4) for what I desire for you. Freedom, peace, joy, and happiness. For I am the Master of Happiness. And you are sharing in my happiness.

Gold Chalice

This is what the Lord says ... I have placed in you a gold chalice. The chalice has come from me. Inside this chalice, there is liquid gold. This gold will pour out of your mouth. But it will not just pour out from your mouth, it will pour out of all parts of you. It will pour out of your body, and every cell in your body will be infused with this liquid gold. My healing power for the mental, the physical, and the emotional, every part of the mind, body, and soul. This gold is bubbling up, and it is heating up, and it will overflow.

My chalice will overflow from within you. It is coming to a heating point, a bubbling-over point, from which will flow revelation, healing power, insight, visions, and wisdom. It will flood all parts of your life. And from you, that gold will seep out, touching other people's souls. It will change lives; just a drop of that gold will change people's lives. The gold and revelation will bubble up and flow out of you like a flood.

Everywhere you go, every person will be touched, whether you see it or not; something will happen. Their spirit will connect to your spirit, that liquid gold will touch everything, everything you say—there will be liquid gold upon it. Even if they're just normal words you speak, they will be coated with the anointing. For I have placed in you this chalice, and you have filled it up and filled it up with my Word, and soon it will overflow.

Your Journey – Step Number Seven

As you plant the seed of the Word of God in your heart and water it with worship, it will grow. Just as a seed is planted in the ground, it is changing and developing deep in the soil before any shoots break through the earth. It is the same with the Word of God within you, changes will begin to happen on the inside. Then a time will come when the shoot appears, and eventually it will grow into a plant which bears fruit. Then there will be an overflow from the inside to the outside. Continue to record your journey with the Lord by reviewing the questions in the Bonus gift and recognizing the gifts of abundance the Lord has already blessed you with on the inside.

Chapter 8

Goodness and Love – Blessings Follow Me Always

Psalm 23:6

"Surely your goodness and love will follow me all the days of my life . . . "

When I was a young Christian and first heard Bible teacher Stephen O' Brien say, "the words you speak today are the footpath you walk on tomorrow," I wasn't convinced! I couldn't understand how I could have such influence over events in my own life. I had always felt life was something that happened to me, and I just got dragged along! But I decided I was going to find out for myself.

I made a list of all the areas in my life that needed a significant Godly intervention. It was a long list! Then I got a notebook and searched the internet for Bible scriptures on health, finances, family, work, whatever I could think of—I searched for it. I chose scriptures that really impacted me, and I began to declare the Word was true and whatever God promised me in the Bible belonged to me.

Unexpected things began to happen. The Lord began to rebuild my life to accommodate the blessings he wanted to bring me. I would meet people who were of great encouragement to me. Anywhere I went, I had great peace and enjoyed the Lord's company. Our Father in heaven doesn't forget anything. As a child, I always loved dogs, and the Lord blessed me with a gorgeous Cavachon puppy named Daisy. I had also always wanted to go horse riding, and in my fiftieth year, I began horse riding.

"Take delight in the LORD, and he will give you the desires of your heart." (Psalm 37:4)

We might have a list of blessings we would like our Father to provide, such as a bigger house or a new car. But he may have a different list of blessings he wants to give us first. He may be blessing you in an amazing way, but he may not have revealed to you the potential of that blessing.

When I prayed with people and received these beautiful verses that fill this book, I couldn't see the book. I just knew I was blessed to receive them and blessed to share them with the person I was praying for. In scripture, a master speaks to his servant, just as our Father speaks to us. As we are faithful to the Word in small things, the Lord will open a door where we can be faithful in many things.

"His master replied, 'Well done, good and faithful servant! You have been faithful with a few things; I will put you in charge of many things. Come and share your master's happiness.'" (Matthew 25:21)

Letter to Heaven

This is what the Lord says ... I opened an envelope, and the letter was written by you to me. But your letter contains my Words, my Words which glorify me. It fills my heart to hear you speak to me that way. When you declare you are blessed and have received from me in the spirit, I can release those blessings from your belly. Your words trigger these blessings. Heaven rejoices when my children are blessed. Your words are spirit and are in written form in spirit. When you speak my words, the written words in the spirit are addressed to me.

Endless Capacity to Give

This is what the Lord says ... I hear you call on me, calling me into every situation, every question, every decision. I enjoy being part of your life so much. I eagerly look to my other children for them to call on me. You are like an only child. I have so many gifts and blessings for all my children, but they go unused. Therefore, I flood you with them. I give them all to you because I see you enjoy them and want to use them. I have an endless capacity to give. It gives me great pleasure to give to you. Continue to surrender to me, and I will continue to fill you up with my gifts and blessings. The greater the availability within you, the greater my capacity to supply.

Safe Hands

This is what the Lord says ... My eyes see everything. My ears hear everything. I am doing a new thing here. It is hidden from you, but soon it will be revealed. Fear not, for you are in my hand. And I will not let you fall. My hand only lifts up, never brings down.

Ups and Downs

This is what the Lord says ... You go up and down. I am in the ups and downs. I am in the ins and outs. I steadfastly stand by you. I am always there. I have nurtured and fed you to grow into me. And as you grow into me, I can then grow into you. You are blessed beyond many. Because you ask and want to receive, I will continue to bless you.

Blanket of Love

This is what the Lord says ... I am the blanket of love that surrounds you. The enemy may surround you, engulf you. It is a blanket that warms you in the difficult times, but you can cool down in the best of times. For my love, though always there, ebbs and flows within your life according to what you declare. It is a living, vibrant blanket I give from my heart to serve you.

Umbrella

This is what the Lord says ... I cover you with the palm of my hand. I hold you in the palm of my hand. For my child, I provide all—all protection, all needs, all desires, all gifts. I cocoon you in my hands like a delicate flower, letting no weapon harm you. If you step away from me and out of my palm, you leave my protection. Pay attention to the atmosphere around you and every place you set your foot. When you take me everywhere you go, you take my umbrella of protection with you. When you are under my umbrella, it rains down blessings from the inside and protects against the rain from the world. My strong tower is always available to you to shelter in.

Life from Life

This is what the Lord says ... You were birthed out of me, and I am going to birth a blessing out of you. I've set the path before you. I have shown you the way. In due time, I will be seen. All around you, the enemy is screaming at you to come off your path. But you stand firm. This pregnancy will come to an end, and when it does, the miracle of life will be revealed. For life breeds life, only from life can life come. I have made all things with life, so I have supplied all that you need. Don't look to the dead things, but look to the living. My will is from life, life will come.

Birthing Blessings

This is what the Lord says ... I have blessed you beyond many because you allow me to. These blessings have been birthed in you. Now they will come out of you as a child will come out of you. The blessings will be a strong tower for you and many others. They will be the evidence that I am alive and a loving Father. The love for my people will pour out of you. There will be no question amongst the people who you are, but the Pharisees will reject you as much as they can. But fear not, for Jesus always has the victory. Many of my children will come home to me because of you.

Rest

This is what the Lord says ... I love you, my child. You are a part of my heart. My heart is for the people. You yearn for them as I yearn for them to turn to their father and draw off me. To draw the strength, the love, the tenacity they need to survive. As many turned away from Jesus, many turn away from you. But I see your struggle, your struggle to impart my Word. But I do not ask you to struggle, I ask you to rest. There are other workers out there who I have called to me. They are hidden in me, and you do not see them. But I see them. It is not all on your shoulders. It is all on my shoulders. No more struggle, rest in me now. Always resting. Bless you, my child of light.

Puppy Love

This is what the Lord says ... Today, I give you a gift of a puppy. But this puppy is not for you to keep. It is a gift to give. I give many people "gifts to give," but they keep them instead, when that is not the purpose. It is important to know when it's a gift to keep and when it's a gift to give. In the spirit, I have many more gifts for you and for others. These are not just any gifts but are gifts with blessings, *spiritual* blessings. It takes a sharp ear and discernment, an open heart to know when it is a gift to keep and when it is a gift to give.

Supernatural Wealth

This is what the Lord says ... I have opened up your heart like a flower. Now I open up your hand to receive what I have to give you. I have painstakingly removed the thorns from your heart, and it throbs in beat with mine. Now I will release the worldly ways from your hand. And as you hold my hand, supernatural wealth will flow from me to you. Freedom in all areas of your life is about to manifest. You have freedom in your spirit, and the words you have spoken will become flesh, it will manifest in the physical.

Freedom from Toil

This is what the Lord says ... I raise you up in the morning, and I lay you down to rest in the evening. Throughout the day, you visit with me often. But I long for you to visit and stay with me all the time. For the decisions you make, I want to be involved. I want to guide and keep you safe, blessed, and prosperous. For my son is not made to toil, but to fellowship with me so that I, as your Father, can lay the path of peace, joy, and freedom—freedom from all toil so that you are blessed in all areas of your life.

Song of life

This is what the Lord says ... I am in tune with you, and you are in tune with me. As the tune goes up and down, I am with you in the melody. I write the song, and you sing it. You follow my music, and I enjoy listening to you. You are creative in your own right, but you look to me, which I love and enjoy. You could sing your own song, but you sing mine. Sometimes the song is difficult for you, but you press into it to do it right. All those years, I listened to you playing the piano. Now you are listening to me. You will go on and on listening to me, becoming more and more skilled, refining your ability. It is a pleasure for me to sing this song with you.

Pearl

This is what the Lord says ... My beautiful daughter, I named you Pearl. You have been formed due to the pressure of the world. The greater the pressure, the more you have come to me. Out of the ashes, I have created great beauty. "… The kingdom of heaven is like a merchant looking for fine pearls. When he found one of great value, he went away and sold everything he had and bought it." (Matthew 13:45)

Provider

This is what the Lord says ... I am like your horse that carries you. I am like your puppy who cuddles and kisses you. I am the gardener who grows the plants for you. I am the farmer who raises the cattle for you. I am the butcher who cuts the meat for you. I am the fisherman who catches the fish for you. I am the dressmaker who sews the clothes for you. I am the shoemaker who makes the shoes for you. You are surrounded by me in service to you. For I draw out of all these people wells of service to you and my children. I am the great provider for whatever you need. I will provide. I supply all your needs. I give you the desires of your heart.

Unexpected Gifts

This is what the Lord says ... I rise within you, becoming more and more established. You give me presence. You give me the channel through which I operate. We are a team operating in tandem. For some time now, I have watched you grow and change. As this continues, new elements of my presence will be revealed to you. Unexpected gifts will come naturally out of your spirit. You will recognize them as from me.

Gardener in Heaven

This is what the Lord says ... I am blessing you with heavenly blessings. Those prayer requests that you made to me. I have heard them all. You send your prayer with the power of my Word behind it and with your faith delivering it. The shoots have come through the soil, but the fruit is just a season away. You will begin to see the evidence of the shoots in your life. New things will happen. I will be there every step of the way, guiding you, for I have orchestrated this garden of shoots to grow up around you, as I am the gardener in heaven.

Heaven's Clock

This is what the Lord says ... I unveil your heart, and I unveil his heart at the designated time. I am pruning and preparing his heart, as I have prepared your heart. It will happen, but on heaven's time. When heaven's clock beats on Earth, the alarm will go off, and you will know it's time. He will know it's time for the union to take place. Nothing in your life is left to chance. My hand is on all things in your life. For you have invited me in and declared my word. It is all established in the heavens.

Your Journey – Step Number Eight

God's goodness and love can be seen in the form of blessings in our lives. They are the fulfillment of God's promises to us. They are already established in the spirit realm before we see them in the physical realm. However, opportunities or people may enter our lives and appear to be a blessing but may not be.

Many people make decisions without seeking counsel from the Holy Spirit. They may go down a career path or get married in complete confidence that this is the right decision. But over time, it may be revealed that the career was not the right one or the person was not the right person for them.

If you seek the Lord prior to making decisions and ask him to reveal to you any hidden pits, then he will guide you accordingly and his goodness and love will prevail in all circumstances. Ask him to close the doors he doesn't want you to go through, to remove the people he doesn't want in your life, and to bring the opportunities and people he does want in your life. Continue recording your journey with the Lord by showing gratitude for the blessings you already have and by reviewing the questions in the Bonus gift.

Chapter 9

Dwell in the House of the Lord – Family Reunited

Psalm 23:6

"And I will dwell in the house of the Lord forever."

At seventeen years of age, I gave my life to God while seeking him for direction after leaving school. By receiving Jesus, I became a child of God. "Yet to all who did receive him, to those who believed in his name, he gave the right to become children of God." (1 John 1:12) However, I did not know that if I read the Bible, I could get to know Jesus.

It was many decades later that I received the Holy Spirit. In John 14:15, Jesus said, "If you love me, keep my commands. And I will ask the Father, and he will give you another advocate to help you and be with you forever—the Spirit of truth." Then I really sought out the Lord in his Word and found John 14:23, "Jesus replied, 'Anyone who loves me will obey my teaching. My Father will love them, and we will come to them and make our home with them.'"

I became the house in which God the Father, Jesus, and the Holy Spirit live, as described in Hebrews 3:6b "And we are his house ..." and Romans 8:38-39, "For I am convinced that neither death nor life, neither angels nor demons, neither the present nor the future, nor any powers, neither height nor depth, nor anything else in all creation, will be able to separate us from the love of God that is in Christ Jesus our Lord."

He will live inside you, too, and you will never be separated again from the love of the Father.

Jesus the Victor

This is what the Lord says ... My heart is open for all my children. Many believe I don't care, and I neglect them. But I have given my only begotten son that I may reunite with my lost children. Jesus is the doorway back into the garden with me, the pathway to my throne in the kingdom, the bread that feeds you, the water that refreshes you. He is everything you need, only through him can you survive spiritually. Do not look to the right or left. Just look at him.

Jesus is peace. Jesus is freedom. Jesus is healing. Jesus is redemption. Jesus is eternal life. Jesus is a loving son and a loving brother. Many sons have gone to war and fought against terrible armies. My Son went to war alone and faced all the armies of hell on his own. They took him, imprisoned him, and inflicted great torment on him. However, my Son, Jesus, is freedom and could never be bound. His sacrifice will be celebrated for eternity.

Part of the Family

This is what the Lord says ... My precious child, I knitted you in your mother's womb. (Psalm 139:13) I placed in you a treasure buried within your spirit. No eye has seen, no ear has heard, no human mind has conceived the things I have prepared for you. (1 Corinthians 2:9) As you have spoken the Word over many years, it has removed layer after layer of debris from this world that has covered the treasure.

Please do not stop now, my child, though you may grow weary, do not give up. For at the proper time, you will reap a harvest. (Galatians 6:9) Though you may think nobody needs you, the body of Christ needs you. You are a member of that body. Without a foot, the body is lame, without a leg, it stumbles. Without ears, it cannot hear, without eyes, it cannot see. Thus, if one part suffers, all the parts suffer with it. The body of Christ suffers without you. Return to the family where they honor you, and all members share in your happiness.

Family Crest

This is what the Lord says ... Whatever day you wake up, whatever hour you draw closer to me, I see you in all your glory, your spiritual glory. My light shines through you. You are ever seeking me in all situations. I delight to be part of your struggle and joy from this day onwards. A new light will rest on you and shine through you. It is a new anointing cloak made of oil. The majesty of this cloak is seen in the spirit world. You are wearing the cloak I wear. Just like a family crest, this is our family crest.

Paternal Protector

This is what the Lord says ... I delight in my children. I delight in my daughter's coming together and blessing each other. When together as a family with me, I will bless you each in abundance. I crave to spend time with my family. I long to hear you speak to me and I to you. My family is growing, and so are you, spiritually. Don't be afraid to come to me with everything. Remember, I am the strong tower in which you can shelter. I am the feathers that cover you. I go before you. I am above you and below you. I am behind you. No one can get you unless they come through me. I am your eternal paternal protector.

Valentine

This is what the Lord says ... You are my Valentine. I am your Valentine. Your name is written on my heart. There is no greater gift I can give you than my love. You have delighted in my Son, Jesus, unlike any other. And I will give you the desires of your heart, (Psalm 37:40) even the secret things you have in your heart. Some of you have asked me for and some of you have not.

But I see them all and will give you all you ask and all you haven't asked. For I know you inside and out, and I'm eager to give you all. Do not be forlorn and look to the past. Look ahead, for that is where all the treasures are laid out for you. Your life will turn a corner, and you will see what you've spoken. You are not just my Valentine on this day but my Valentine every minute of every day. Love, your Dad.

Happy Birthday

This is what the Lord says to you ... The angels so rejoiced in heaven when you were born many years ago. I had marked you out long before you were born to do great and mighty things for me. But it is not what you do for me that pleases me most. It is that you are such a loving son to me, always looking to be close to me and to please me. You do please me greatly. You sit here with me, day after day, night after night, cushioned within the bosom of my spirit. I have sent you forth as a good shepherd to gather my children to me.

You send out my Word as your brother, Jesus, did. You lay hands on the sick as your brother, Jesus, did. You teach my children about me as your brother, Jesus, did. You cast out demons as your brother, Jesus, did. You are close to the brokenhearted as Jesus was. You cry with those who cry and rejoice with those who rejoice. You are my image and likeness. I know you will never leave me or forsake me. This gives me great comfort and reassurance. You are my great reward, my eternal joy. For I know through you Jesus still walks on the Earth. Happy birthday, my beloved child.

Blossoming

This is what the Lord says ... My flower, you are blossoming. Each petal reveals Jesus within you. I am stretching you in spirit, and you submit willingly to my calling. You are such a loving daughter to me and a loving sister to Jesus. I wait at night and into the morning for you to wake, so you may chat with me and take me with you throughout your day. I take delight in you, and you give me the desires of my heart.

Joy-filled Heart

This is what the Lord says ... My dear child, I have been waiting for you to come to me for so long. You have filled my heart with joy, now you have come into the family. The angels of heaven rejoice that my child has been found. Now that I walk hand in hand with you everywhere you go, I will never leave you nor forsake you. (Hebrews 13:5) I go before you. I stand behind you. I surround you. Lay your burdens on me that you may be free. You have my coat of love, and you will always have it until you return one day to the bosom of my spirit in heaven.

Original Plan

This is what the Lord says ... I rise within you. I go forth through you. I lay my hands through your hands. I walk through your feet. I speak through your mouth. You have surrendered yourself to me. And as you continue to do so, I am the greater part of you, though you may seem to be losing yourself. You are, in fact, just hiding within me. You will have silver and gold, and all the treasures in heaven are available to you. You are dressed in fine robes—your hair, like waves of the sea. And everywhere you go, the queen I have grown you up to be will be seen everywhere. People will be astonished and follow you to get to me, bringing my children home, as was my original plan.

Heaven's Court

This is what the Lord says ... The Lord is Judge. One by one, people come before him. The first person to be tried, the Judge halts the proceedings and tells the accused that if they have chosen Jesus on earth, he will do the sentence for their crime. The accused has accepted Jesus. The Judge then invites the free accused to come and live with him in his mansion. The love of God is boundless!

Waiting in the Garden

This is what the Lord says ... I opened the eyes of the blind, and they opened their hearts to me. In one step, the atmosphere changes instantly, and I bring the Father and the Holy Spirit. We come into the Garden of Eden, for the Father never left the garden but waits there for you to return. It's pleasant in the garden but empty without you. Many walk around the garden but hesitate to enter through the gate. Yet the gate is open, and the Father calls. Few come into the garden, you are entering into the riches of the garden. You are leaving the things of the world and stepping in—with every step, a step closer to the Father.

Heavenly Retirement

This is what the Lord says ... Heaven is home for me and my children. It is pain-free, trouble-free, full of peace, joy, and righteousness. The earth is the battleground, but heaven is protected from earthly things. It is like a retirement home, but for the forever young. You will see so much and learn so much that you will never be bored. I wait daily for my children to come home.

Going Home

This is what the Lord says ... My child, my child, how I delight in you. Delight, you have returned to the kingdom, to the family in heaven. You will rest here in me in the bosom of my spirit for all eternity. Reunited with family who have gone before you, your parents, and grandparents. How the heavens rejoice when a son comes home to stay! A banquet is laid out, and everyone rejoices. The angels sing "Glory to God," and my prayer is answered when a child comes home.

Your Journey - Step Number Nine

Many walk the road of life without the Lord. It may look blessed on the outside, with all the trimmings of the world. But there is a vacancy, an ache on the inside that can only be filled by the love of our heavenly Father. We are made in his image and likeness; he knows what you need and desire and longs to give it to you. You belong in the family surrounded by the family members—your heavenly Father, brother Jesus, and the teacher, the Holy Spirit, who will teach you all things about the family. Conclude your "Journey through the valley of darkness" by recording what it would mean to you to have the assurance that one day, you know you will return to heaven and rest your head on heaven's pillow.

Conclusion

Your Journey - Step Number Ten

I hope this book has been a wonderful, special experience for you with the Lord and not just a book you read. I hope that you have felt the presence of the Lord and your heart has been touched by his Words, through which he has poured out his love. Now that you have tasted the love our heavenly Father has for you, you know you are safe with him, safe to come to him. The Lord has called you to be close to him, to allow him into your life.

Wherever you are in the journey of life, if you are in the valley of darkness, you don't have to travel alone. At your request, Jesus will come, hold your hand, be your shepherd, and light up the road of life. No evil will you fear. Just say this short prayer, "Lord Jesus, you died for my sins, please come into my heart, be my savior and Lord."

Congratulations! You are now in the family of God, and your name has been written in the Book of Life in heaven. You are no longer lost but found. No longer on life's path struggling on your own, but now have the company of God the Father, Jesus, and the Holy Spirit. Whatever happens in your life from this moment on can be a different experience from what it has been before.

To bring the kingdom into your daily life on earth, Jesus, the Word of God, must be Lord of your life. In the kingdom, the currency is faith, which comes from hearing the Word. The Bible is the manual on how to live a blessed life. Jesus will restore your soul, heal your wounds. He will lead you on a path of protection, blessings, and victory. He will anoint your head with oil, reveal the plans he has for you, and your cup will overflow. When the number of your days on this earth has been fulfilled, Jesus will be waiting to welcome you home into the Kingdom, to live there forever.

To continue on this journey, join me at:

www.holyspiritbooks.org
youtube.com/@jesusfaithwarrior

Acknowledgments

Many people have contributed to the formation of this book directly and indirectly over many years. Acknowledging everyone is impossible, but I would like to thank the key contributors.

Thank you to my family, particularly my parents who provided endless opportunities and supported me in my many endeavors over many years.

I want to thank Stephen O' Brien, whose Bible teaching I have sat under for over a decade. Stephen's teaching ignited a hunger in me for the Word of God that I didn't even know I had, an exceptional teacher. Stephen has also been a steadfast friend, confidant, and support throughout the countless battles I have endured. Thank you also, Stephen, for writing the Foreword for this book. I appreciate it.

Thank you to James and Liz McCann who opened their door to give our little Church a home, where everyone is fed the Word of God by Stephen, and people go home satisfied. It has been an honor and a privilege to frequent your home, a special place to support and encourage each other.

I want to thank Ivan Nixon, a humble man of God whom the Lord greatly used on my first encounter with the Holy Spirit.

Always very encouraging and supportive throughout my walk with the Lord.

Thank you, Margaret Moore, a wonderful, loyal, steadfast, and supportive friend with a heart of pure gold.

Thank you to Myron Golden, who through his You Tube channel and "Make More Offers Challenge" has been a cornerstone in the process by which I have stepped into the business world. I asked God to send me a business teacher who knew him, and he brought Myron onto my path. Myron's ability to teach business according to Biblical principles has been an incredible revelation and has given me great peace to know God operates in my business.

I want to thank Eleanor Manning, a wonderful friend who has given me incredible encouragement and shared in the excitement of this adventure.

Thank you to Chad Gilmer, Adrian Crilly and David Murphy (photographer) all incredibly talented and creative, who took my vision of an old book shop and gave it life, creating an incredible brand and website for Holy Spirit Books (www.holyspiritbooks.org). A home for *If God were to Speak to You.*

Thank you to Irene Regan, a great friend for many years for proofreading this book.

A special thank you to Shanda Trofe for her professional publishing guidance and support throughout the process. Thank you particularly for your patience in answering my many questions.

Most importantly, I would like to acknowledge the readers of this book. Many of you may have been skeptical at the beginning of this book, but you have made it all the way to the end. Even if you only had faith as small as a seed, it was still a seed. I hope that seed has been nourished in reading this book, for it has been written for you.

About the Author

Fidelma Hernon B.Sc., M.Sc., Ph.D., has worked as a research scientist, medical scientist, and surveillance scientist. Fidelma views science as the study of God's creation. From a young child seeking God in the woodlands next to her childhood home, she has sought him in all her life's decisions, asking him to close the doors he doesn't want her to go through and open the doors he does want her to go through.

Fidelma was diligent in her studies in school and loves music, with a desire to have a career in music, obtaining teacher diplomas in piano and elocution. However, God closed those doors and opened the door into science, although she didn't demonstrate any scientific ability at school. When in college, God revealed a natural scientific ability in her. This led her to study God's brilliant creation through science in Microbiology.

Living abroad and traveling extensively has been a wonderful exposure to different cultures and countries that Fidelma has enjoyed.

Through her scientific accomplishments, she has many years of experience presenting to large groups of well-informed people.

Fidelma currently resides in Dublin, Ireland, and enjoys working out, cycling, walking her dog Daisy, and horse riding.

As Fidelma grew in faith, the Lord began to draw new gifts out of her, a gift of teaching and a gift of prophecy. She began teaching the Bible in her workplace, and lives have been changed through these teachings.

Fidelma is now excited to share this book with the world and tell the lost people that God knows who you are and wants to talk to you.

Printed in Dunstable, United Kingdom

70222135R00077